STEP IN TO RECOVERY SERIES

D0448541

Step Up

Unpacking Steps One, Two, and Three
with Someone Who's Been There

MICHAEL GRAUBART

Hazelden
Publishing

Hazelden Publishing
Center City, Minnesota 55012
hazelden.org/bookstore

Library of Congress Cataloging-in-Publication Data
Names: Graubart, Michael, 1958- author.
Title: Step up : unpacking steps one, two, and three with someone who's been there / Michael Graubart.
Description: Center City, Minnesota : Hazelden Publishing, [2017] |
    Series: Step in to recovery series | Includes bibliographical references.
Identifiers: LCCN 2017025231 (print) | LCCN 2017029961 (ebook) |
ISBN 9781616497477 (ebook) | ISBN 9781616497460 (softcover)
Subjects: LCSH: Twelve-step programs. | Recovering alcoholics. | Recovering addicts.
Classification: LCC HV5276 (ebook) | LCC HV5276 .G73 2017 (print) |
    DDC 616.86/06--dc23
LC record available at https://lccn.loc.gov/2017025231

Editor's note

This publication is intended to support personal growth and should not be thought of as a substitute for the advice of health care professionals. The author's advice and viewpoints are his own.

Some names, details, and circumstances may have been changed to protect the privacy of those mentioned in this publication.

Alcoholics Anonymous, AA, and the Big Book are registered trademarks of Alcoholics Anonymous World Services, Inc. Hazelden Publishing offers a variety of information on addiction and related areas. The views and interpretations expressed herein are those of the author and are neither endorsed nor approved by AA or any Twelve Step organization.

21 20 19 18 17   1 2 3 4 5 6

Cover design: Kathi Dunn, Dunn + Associates
Typesetting: Percolator
Development editor: Vanessa Torrado

Dedicated to the men who sponsored me
over my first twenty-five years in Alcoholics Anonymous
Bob S., Charlie M., Hal R., and Milton D.

*If you can stay sober in Alcoholics Anonymous,
you can stay sober anywhere.**

---

* Or clean in Narcotics Anonymous or abstinent in Overeaters
Anonymous, or whichever "A" applies to you.

IN THIS BOOK

Part 2: Stepping It Up:
Taking Steps One, Two, and Three

Part 3: Questions People Often Ask
in Early Twelve Step Recovery

An Invitation to Another Way of Life

This book is a guide for people who wish to *get* or *stay* sober, to *find* or *deepen* their recovery through Twelve Step practices. Together, we'll cover everything you need for a strong understanding of Twelve Step recovery and the program's first three Steps.

These Steps serve as the foundation of Alcoholics Anonymous (AA), Narcotics Anonymous (NA), Marijuana Anonymous (MA), Cocaine Anonymous (CA), Al-Anon, Overeaters Anonymous (OA), Debtors Anonymous (DA), and any other program ending in "A." So, the goal is to give you a strong foundation for another way of life.

I'll also give you an idea of what to expect—and demand—when you come to a Twelve Step fellowship. The operative phrase, as with everything in the fellowship: "Take what you like and leave the rest."

This book is neither Conference-approved nor politically correct.

It represents the experience, strength, and hope of exactly one sober alcoholic who desires to share the good news of Twelve Step recovery—that there is a solution, and that you never have to drink, use, or be lonely again—if you're willing to follow our proven path.

•

The book has a second goal as well.

The Second Step invites the recovering alcoholic and addicts to be restored to sanity.

After twenty-five years of continuous sobriety and active membership in the AA fellowship, my belief is that while Twelve Step recovery has traditionally been rooted in a spiritual program, we've gotten off course. Things have *gone insane*. Know that while my word choice might feel harsh, there's a very particular reason I'm using the term *insane*.* The Second Step invites recovering addicts and alcoholics to be restored to *sanity* through the belief of a Power greater than ourselves—and, as an extension, through *the practice of a spiritual program*. Yet, many aspects of how the fellowship functions today have moved away from *the very thing* that was supposed to help us all restore our sanity: *spirituality*.

Twelve Step recovery has entered a post-spiritual phase. My perspective is that we need to embrace the program as it was meant to be lived.

The program was developed many decades ago; since that time, our society, culture, norms, and even our vocabulary have all evolved. Terminology in use since the earliest days of the Twelve Step program is challenging for many people to approach. I'm not saying or implying that we should all go back in time for our sobriety; what I am saying is that in our evolution, we've lost hold of a vital part of the program that really can transcend everything—including our addictions. And that's the *spiritual*.

Many meetings today are essentially group therapy without a therapist. These meetings consist of a mishmash of complaining about life, therapy-speak, treatment center concepts, updates on the health of the members' cats, and "checking in about my day" or "claiming my seat." There's almost nothing about the joy of recovery, the relief from the bondage of alcoholism and addiction, or the spirituality of the program.

Newcomers get the idea that telling the group about how your cat is doing and claiming one's seat is Twelve Step recovery, and there are people who have been working a program for a while who assume *that's all there is to it*.

It's not.

---

*We'll discuss the concept of insanity in greater detail when we cover the Steps.

The problem that brings us to any Twelve Step fellowship is a spiritual problem, one we've tried and failed to solve with alcohol, drugs, sex, food, money, debting, spending, over-exercising, smoking, or a host of other behaviors. In the simplest terms, we addicts feel a *hole* in our lives, an absence of something in our sense of self, in our being. To fill that hole, we use substances, people, or money (that we have, that we don't have, or that other people have). We use because we have lost or never found a connection to something bigger than ourselves.

The problem we share is *spiritual*; which is why the essence of the solution is also spiritual.

I've been at countless meetings during which people read from the spiritual language in the Big Book, Basic Text, or other Conference-approved sources. Once read, the ideas are often ignored, as if they were a meaningless hangover from an earlier time, and the meeting goes on to how everyone's cats are and claiming one's seat.

So let's get real.

To get and stay clean and sober, or to find recovery in any fellowship, you don't have to adopt the word *God* or the word *Creator* or any other term for a Higher Power. The term is not the point.

If you want the full benefit of recovery, and not just the physical sobriety you can achieve solely by going to meetings, you've got to find a Power greater than yourself.

Without that Power, there's no real change of heart, thought, or behavior. Without that Power, we're not in touch with the spiritual.

We remain the person we were when locked in our addiction.

We never get to find out who we could have been.

That's what Twelve Step recovery traditionally helped people do—find that Power greater than themselves and live the lives that they were always meant to live.

Twelve Step recovery is a coin with two sides—the first is the *fellowship;* the second is the *recovery program* itself. My hope is that by refocusing on the spiritual nature of the solution to addiction, this book will help refocus on the goals of the program and restore the fellowship, and not just individual alcoholics and addicts, to sanity.

It's a big wish, but both the newcomer and the old-timer deserve nothing less.

•

The book is divided into three sections, and each one is written in question-answer format to address the queries I've most frequently heard from newcomers to Twelve Step recovery. The first section introduces you to the concept of Twelve Step recovery in general. The second takes you through the first three Steps. And the third covers the most common issues that addicts and alcoholics have once they begin their recovery.

PART 1

Now What?

You're thinking maybe you need some
sort of help to get or stay clean and
sober . . . so what are you going to find
in Twelve Step recovery? What are the
meetings like? Is it really for you?

Q. What Are Twelve Step Programs? Are They Cults?

A. Twelve Step recovery groups describe themselves as *fellowships*. The word is well chosen—it means that there is no leadership, no elected officials, no political parties, no dues or fees to pay.

Twelve Step recovery is also not a religion. You can remain a member of your religion, or you can have no religion in your life, and still have the Twelve Steps work for you.

Twelve Step programs are peer-to-peer entities in which no member is more important than any other. Everyone in a Twelve Step fellowship has the same basic goals—to stop drinking, drugging, spending, overeating, or whatever; to stay stopped; and to live a better, more fulfilling life. That's it.

Sometimes people worry that Twelve Step fellowships might be cults, especially when they go to meetings and see other people reciting rote phrases like some bad 1950s sci-fi film about brainwashing.

Consider this: If the fellowships were cults, they would specialize in recruiting new members who still had money in the bank, two cars in the garage, and a steady income. But that's not how it works. Most people have to lose everything, or almost everything—their careers, their relationships, their dignity, their savings, sometimes even their freedom—before they are willing to come to a meeting. If Twelve Step programs were self-serving cults, they wouldn't recruit people who had nothing left in the bank!

You will undoubtedly find people who want to be considered powerful and important within the fellowship. But as it's been said, "Wanting to be important in AA is like wanting to be head leper in a leper colony." A healthier approach is to believe in another expression: "AA is not my whole life, but it makes my life whole." ■

Q. Where Did Twelve Step Programs Come From?

A. The first fellowship (or program) was AA, which came into existence when its cofounders, Bill Wilson and Dr. Bob Smith, met in a manner that seems—to most people in recovery—an act of Divine Providence.*

Bill W., as we still refer to him, was a severely alcoholic Wall Street type who had found a spiritual solution to his alcoholism. He was a few months sober when he traveled from his home in Brooklyn, New York, to Akron, Ohio, in the spring of 1935 to oversee one side of a proxy battle for control of a local company. Bill's side lost, and he was stuck in Akron for a weekend with nothing to do and nothing to show for the time he and others had invested in the project.

That Saturday afternoon, he paced the lobby floor, peering into his hotel's bar, where people were enjoying themselves drinking. The temptation he felt to join them was unbearable.

Fortunately for him (and for us), Bill did not succumb. Instead, he relied on the solution to his drinking problem that he had hit upon in previous months in New York—to find other alcoholics and talk to them about sobriety.

Bill hadn't been very successful in New York, going into barrooms and preaching the joys of not drinking to men who were

___

*While the practice is to protect one's anonymity in Twelve Step programs, I'm using the full names for Bill Wilson, Dr. Bob Smith, and also Lois Wilson and Ebby Thatcher, because these individuals are historic figures and are often named in full in Twelve Step circles.

sitting on their barstools, nursing their beers. He might not have kept anyone else sober, but the process of discussing his alcoholism had kept him from touching alcohol for many months.

Bill decided to change his approach. Stuck in a hotel for the weekend, far from home, Bill set out to find an alcoholic in Akron with whom he could discuss sobriety.

But how do you find a drunk in a city not your home? This was Bill's dilemma. He noticed a listing of clergymen on a wall in the lobby near a pay phone. Bill went down the list of clergymen, calling ten of them, asking them if they knew any alcoholics with whom he could work.

Imagine for a moment that you were one of those clergymen. It's a nice spring afternoon, you have concluded religious services, and you are now enjoying lunch with your family and perhaps a few parishioners. And then you get a call, out of the blue, from a stranger who tells you that he is an alcoholic from New York, and he wonders if you know any alcoholics with whom he could talk.

What do you do?

You hang up on him.

Such was Bill's experience with the first nine clergymen he called. Then he dropped his tenth nickel into the phone and reached a pastor named Reverend Walter Tunks. Bill explained his mission.

Tunks knew an alcoholic.

"Let me get back to you," Reverend Tunks replied.

The alcoholic in question was Dr. Bob Smith, a surgeon and proctologist whose drinking problem was legendary in Akron medical circles. He would show up at the hospital, drink a bottle of beer to steady his nerves, and then go operate. Bill was looking for a practicing alcoholic who needed to get sober; Dr. Bob, Tunks knew, was just such a man.

Reverend Tunks reached out to an Akron woman, Henrietta Sieberling, heiress to a tire fortune. She knew Dr. Bob. The good reverend explained about the mysterious visitor from New York and his desire to reform a local drunk. Dr. Bob, inebriated much of the time, was living in her guest house. She somehow got the doctor to commit to a fifteen-minute visit with Bill, in her guest house. The visit actually had to be postponed briefly, because Dr. Bob was as drunk as a skunk.

Bill and Dr. Bob finally met. By then, Bill had been cautioned by a man we will come to know better in these pages, Dr. William Silkworth, who ran a drying-out hospital for alcoholics on Manhattan's West Side, not to preach at alcoholics but instead to win their trust by talking about the nature of living as an alcoholic.

This is decades before Oprah. People—especially men—did not share their innermost feelings with one another, especially when the other man was a total stranger. People seldom went to therapy back then. And yet, Bill had the courage to describe to Dr. Bob, in convincing detail, the nature of his alcoholic thinking and actions. Dr. Bob, a physician, had never before encountered anyone who could speak openly and knowledgeably, and from his own personal experience about being addicted to alcohol. That fifteen-minute meeting lasted for six or seven hours.

If only there had been a third party in the room to record and transcribe the conversation! In that discussion, the two men, both small-town New Englanders by birth, both middle-aged, and both familiar with the hopelessness of finding a solution to their drinking problems, talked about the basic idea Bill shared. That idea was that an alcoholic could stay sober through a combination of spirituality (to be explained; stick around) and ongoing contact with fellow problem drinkers.

And thus AA was born, in Akron, Ohio, as a result of a conversation between a New York–based businessman in early sobriety and an Akron-based proctologist who had tried—and failed—to conquer his drinking and was likely on the verge of losing his medical license.

This story is revered in Alcoholics Anonymous and Twelve Step groups, in large measure because of its utter unlikeliness. The whole story is rife with *what ifs*—what if Bill had not gone to Akron for the proxy fight? What if he had won? What if he had succumbed to the temptation of the bar and drowned his self-pity in alcohol? What if he had not thought to call all those clergymen? What if one of the first nine clergymen had offered up an alcoholic other than Dr. Bob? What if Dr. Bob had refused to see him? What if Bill had just decided the whole thing was foolishness and gotten on the first thing smoking, as they talked quaintly about inter-city trains back then, instead of sticking around to meet an Akron drunk?

And yet. If you believe in a Higher Power, or karma, or whatever you want to call it, it's hard not to see the hand of Providence in such a seemingly random encounter. That initial conversation led to a complete transformation of the way the world looks at alcoholism and addiction. Those two strangers, meeting and forming a fast friendship that would last until Dr. Bob's passing sixteen years later, led to an ever-widening circle of individuals finding sobriety—and now, miraculously, that circle includes you.

You are part of that circle no matter what fellowship you are exploring, whether it's AA, NA, Al-Anon, or any of the other more than 200 Twelve Step fellowships that use, with modifications, AA's Twelve Steps. (AA was the first Twelve Step program, which is why some of the other programs use AA language, meeting structure, or literature, in addition to the Steps.)

This is the only disease in the world for which recovery comes from listening to other people tell shockingly funny stories about how insane their lives were. It beats chemo, organ transplantation, and insertion of pacemakers every time. ■

Why Are There Meetings, and Why Do I Have to Go?

A. Alcoholism and addiction are lonely diseases. It's said in meetings that when you are home alone and still a practicing addict or alcoholic, you are behind enemy lines. It's also said that the disease wants to get you alone, so that it can kill you.

As addicts and alcoholics, we often find it very hard to connect on a deep level with other people. We choose the wrong people, bring out the worst in other people, lack the courage to get involved with other people, or simply can't stand other people. Whichever scenario rings true for you, there's a cosmic loneliness inside each of us. Connecting with others in a healthy way is actually a big part of the solution.

AA meetings came about as a means of sharing the method by which alcoholics became and stayed sober, and this is the format that's been followed by every fellowship since. Initially, the first meetings took place in the living room of the home of an early member of AA. At the time, the group didn't even have a formal name. The name Alcoholics Anonymous didn't come about until later. Meetings took place once a week. In order to join, you went over to the home of someone you really didn't know, where the meeting took place. You had to go to one of the upstairs bedrooms with a sober member of the group, and take the first three Steps right then and there. Only then would you be admitted to the meeting.

Many things have changed since then, but the basics have remained the same. Today, if you want to go to a meeting in any fellowship, you just go. No more taking the Third Step prior to the meeting. Search online for a group meeting in your community, and you'll most likely find a meeting list and also a phone number manned by a friendly volunteer who will answer your questions. Today, everyone is welcome at an *open* Twelve Step meeting—sober people, people who are drunk or using (as long as they aren't overly disruptive), friends, family, hostages, observers, *everyone*. (*Open* means that anyone can attend and *closed* means that only individuals who are sober or seeking to become sober are welcome.)

Twelve Step meetings work because pretty much everyone in the room understands why we're all there. We've all been where the newcomer is. We aren't judging you. We're just happy you found us. We know the pain and suffering of active alcoholism and addiction. We understand that alcoholism and addiction are not moral issues. As we say "in the rooms" of recovery, *it's not about bad people becoming good; it's about sick people becoming well.*

There are few places on earth aside from Twelve Step meetings where alcoholics and addicts can talk openly about their "adventures" while drinking and using and still feel accepted and appreciated. Very little goes unsaid or hidden: getting in trouble with the law, losing jobs or careers, destroying marriages and relationships. If anything, when you tell stories like that in a meeting, people love you all the more. (After a while, it's time to tone down the "drunkalogue" or "drugalogue"—but in your earliest days, let it rip.)

In short, meetings provide a safe place for people in recovery to meet, share their experiences, positive and negative, feel better about themselves, feel less lonely, and begin or continue the recovery process.

When AA started, you could only find a meeting in Akron, Ohio, where Bill and Dr. Bob so fortuitously met, or in Manhattan, when Bill returned home. Eventually, people would hear about the program through word of mouth—a doctor in Akron might mention it to a colleague in Columbus, or a person in Chicago might find his way into an Akron meeting. Those individuals took AA and spread it to those other cities. Little by little, meetings grew around the country, and eventually, around the world. As time passed, AA's blueprint for recovery from alcoholism became the road map for the other Twelve Step fellowships.

Today, we take for granted that wherever we are, we can look online and find a comprehensive meeting list with dozens, hundreds, or even thousands of meetings taking place each week within a given locale. Today, we have meetings for men, meetings for women, open meetings, closed meetings (just for those who have acknowledged a problem with alcohol or other drugs), meetings for young people, LGBTQI meetings, meetings in Spanish or Persian, meetings in the United States and across the globe, and so on. It's possible to step off a cruise ship in Alaska and find a meeting in Juneau, catch the meeting, and make it back before the ship sails on. You can find beach meetings in Hawaii. You can find meetings in London, Berlin, and Tokyo. You can find meetings in churches, office buildings, courthouses, police stations, or a thousand other places. In many ways, we just don't realize how lucky we are that the hand of the fellowship is available, pretty much anywhere, anytime.

Just come in, talk to no one if you don't feel like talking, sit in the back and just observe, or if you feel like it, speak at the very first meeting you attend. However you play it, Twelve Step fellowships will welcome you. ■

Q. What Goes On in Meetings?

A. People talk about alcoholism and addiction, about how they recovered from those issues, what they do to stay clean and sober on a daily basis, and sometimes, how their cat is doing.

Every meeting is different. Twelve Step meetings run the gamut from highly disciplined and focused to cocktail-party chatter about how everyone's day went. Some are run democratically, in keeping with the "Traditions" of AA, which we will discuss later in the book. Others, alas, are run by autocratic power trippers who have no life aside from being important in Twelve Step meetings. Every meeting is different because each is a reflection of real life and real people. Will you like everyone you encounter? Probably not. It's said that if you like all the people in all of your meetings, you aren't going to enough meetings.

It's also said that you want to try at least half a dozen different meetings to find the group or groups where you feel most comfortable. As the Twelve Step cliché puts it, "We have a wrench for every nut." ▪

Q. What Do I Have to Do in a Meeting?

A. Nothing.

You will hear suggestions, and it's advisable to follow some or all of the suggestions if you want to stop drinking and using and stay stopped. But as for obligations, the good news is that there are none.

In some meetings, newcomers will be invited to identify themselves, to stand, or to come up and get a "chip and a hug." You don't have to do anything. You can just sit there quietly, minding your own business.

If I could make one change in Twelve Step recovery—words I'll be repeating with some frequency in these pages—I would eliminate the "newcomer chip and a hug." For people who have been to meetings and who have accumulated any amount of clean time, whether it's thirty days or thirty years, the idea of coming back to a meeting and having to go up there for that humiliating "chip and a hug" can be horrifying.

My guess is that the newcomer chip has kept more people from coming back to meetings than anything else on earth. If I ever slip, and I hope I don't, I will sit quietly in the back for as long as it takes until I have the courage to admit that I went out. Please do not ask me to go up in front of the group and publicly admit that I drank again. I couldn't stand the shame, and I truly believe I am not alone.

So don't feel as though you've got to identify yourself in any way. You don't even have to call or label yourself an alcoholic or addict. That's the beauty of the Twelve Step program—you don't *have* to do anything or *be* anyone. Just show up and work the program in the manner that suits you best. (How to do that? Keep reading.)

Come on in; grab a seat in the back. But just come in. You might hear something that transforms your whole life, and you might meet someone who will help save your life.

It happened to me, and to millions of other people. It will work for you, too, if you give it a chance. ■

Q. Michael, What's Your Story?

A. Since you've asked . . .

Okay, you didn't ask, but my editor thought it would make sense to give you a little background. Here goes.

Drank too much. Got fired too often. Got dumped too often. Too much month at the end of the money. Had a good family background and a great education, but that didn't keep me from addiction.

I overcame every advantage on my way to the bottom.

My sisters got me into Al-Anon, where I attended my first meeting on August 25, 1987. A few years later, I got sober.

My last drink to date: January 31, 1992.

So I've been sober for "a few twenty-four hours."

To be honest, I wasn't one of those people who walked in the door and said, "I'm home." Instead, I walked in the door and immediately wanted to walk back out the door.

When I first started attending meetings, it was before that sobriety date I just mentioned. At the time, I really didn't believe I was an alcoholic, and I really wasn't ready to *stop*. I didn't understand what the disease was, and I didn't grasp that I had a problem.

It wasn't until I'd attended enough meetings that I began to recognize how much I really belonged. *I stuck around.* Eventually, as the expression goes, AA ruined my drinking. When that happened, I put my hand up and identified myself as a newcomer.

Then I studied the literature. Did service. Picked up ashtrays and put away chairs. Made coffee. Was secretary. Asked a lot of questions. Found a sponsor and began to sponsor others. Took the Steps. Found a Higher Power. Did jail and prison panels. Went to a ton of meetings.

The usual. ▪

Q. What's the Structure of a Twelve Step Meeting?

A. It varies from meeting to meeting. Some are open, some are closed; some are designed to address the specific needs of certain groups. Some meetings have speakers. Others are discussions during which anyone can speak or "share." Others combine speakers and discussions. Still others study the literature of their particular fellowship or Conference-approved literature. For AA, that includes *Alcoholics Anonymous* (the Big Book), *Twelve Steps and Twelve Traditions* (also known as the 12&12), *Living Sober, As Bill Sees It,* or some other official piece of AA literature. In theory, only *Conference-approved literature*—books that have been published by Alcoholics Anonymous—are studied in AA meetings, but every AA group has the right to set its own rules.

Overeaters Anonymous, Marijuana Anonymous, Cocaine Anonymous, Narcotics Anonymous, Sex and Love Addicts Anonymous, Gamblers Anonymous, Debtors Anonymous, and many other programs also publish their own books and pamphlets. Al-Anon, the fellowship for those affected by the drinking of other people, publishes a great deal of its own material.

Each group's official literature is seen as a vital companion or foundation to understanding and working a program. There are also tons of non-Conference-approved (that means *unofficial*) books, articles, pamphlets, audios, and other materials that make the rounds of meetings. Just because it isn't official doesn't mean it can't be useful.

Since this book is not published by any of the Twelve Step fellowships, strictly speaking, it should not be studied or quoted from in meetings. Of course, if you do quote from it, I promise I won't tell! ▦

Q. Why Are There Steps?

A. It always bothered me that we speak about the Steps in meetings and assume that the newcomer knows what we're talking about. So let's tackle the question of why we have Steps at all, and why we have twelve of them.

There are two aspects of Twelve Step recovery: (1) the *fellowship* and (2) the *recovery program*.

Let's talk about the fellowship first. The fellowship consists of meetings, going out for coffee after the meetings, sponsorship, phoning or texting with members between meetings, and socializing with members between meetings. If you want to check in about your day, or work through a difficult situation you're facing, that's a conversation to have with your sponsor. We carry the mess to our sponsors and we carry the message to our group. Why? Because the newcomer needs to hear about our solutions, not our problems.

We need the fellowship because without it, we are alone in our own heads, and if we are alone, we are, as I mentioned earlier, behind enemy lines. So being part of the fellowship is essential if we intend to stay sober.

The fellowship, however, is not enough. The fact that you go to lots of meetings with a lot of friendly people doesn't mean you'll get or stay clean. The fellowship is necessary but not enough by itself to keep most people sober.

That brings us to the second aspect of Twelve Step recovery: the recovery program. The program is what the Twelve Steps are all about. You take the Steps (this book will explain in detail how to take the first three), and you get better.

So, recovery comes from combining two elements—the fellowship (meetings, sponsorship, contact with people you meet in the meetings) and the recovery program (taking the Steps). ■

Q. What Advice Does the Program Offer about *Stopping*?

A. It's said that all alcoholics eventually stop drinking; the ones who join AA get to stop drinking in their lifetime. If you are reading this book, I'm guessing you are looking for some clarity on how to stop using or drinking—or both.

So how do you do it?

For starters, go to a ton of meetings. When I was newly sober, I had the gift of unemployment, so I made nine meetings a week. How many meetings should you attend? All you can. I once heard a guy say, "I only need one meeting a week, so I go to seven meetings a week, because I never know which one is the meeting I'll need."

Next, consider "people, places, and things." We don't drink or use in a vacuum. There are certain locations that just remind us of getting drunk or high, and you'll want to avoid those if possible. Wherever you used to use or meet your dealer definitely qualifies. So do bars, from dives to seven-star hotels.

We may have drinking or drugging buddies. They are going to laugh at you, be threatened by you, or both if you inform them that you are trying to get clean. Just stay away from them. They will get you high well before you can get them sober.

Things? Maybe it's time to get rid of your wine collection (gasp!). Your bong. Your beer can collection. That little spoon you wear around your neck. You can't keep that stuff in your home and expect that you'll be able to get or stay sober. Need cigarettes? Don't buy them where you used to buy your booze. Delete your dealer's contact from your smartphone (if it were really smart, it would have deleted the contact already).

Get to know people in meetings* and get their phone numbers. Hang around with them before and after meetings. Tell them you're trying to get clean and ask if they can help you.

Get a "sobriety date" and defend it. The day after your most recent use or drink is your sobriety date. Don't just count days and then start over if you pick up. Instead, tattoo your sobriety date on your forehead so everyone can see it. Okay, that last suggestion is just metaphorical. When you have and defend a sobriety date, you are far more likely to stay sober than if you are just "counting days."

Go to the same meetings repeatedly, so that people can get to know you. Big cities offer thousands of meetings per week. Don't be a stranger by going to thirty different meetings in thirty days. Instead, let people get to know you, and you work on getting to know them.

Get a sponsor (about which more later). Just go up to someone who seems remotely sane (again, to avoid possible power differentials and messy relationship issues, look for someone with whom romantic entanglements or sexual motivations will not pop up) and ask, "Will you sponsor me?" You don't have to know what that means, but you'll find out later in the book. The person you ask already knows.

Get to meetings early and don't leave until at least fifteen minutes after the meeting ends. This maximizes the chances of getting to know people in the group, and allowing other people to get to know you.

---

*Ideally, not people to whom you are attracted. Keep your focus. Remember that these meetings are part of working a program for your sobriety and a better way of life. Do everything you can to prevent things from getting romantic, sloppy, and ultimately messy.

Sit up front. They call the back row of meetings the "slipper seats" because that's where people who chronically slip tend to feel comfortable. If you sit up front, you'll catch more of what the speaker has to say. It's not a comedy club—the speaker won't ask where you're from or what you do for work. Trust me, the speaker is only thinking about the speaker.

Ask your Higher Power (more to come on this vital topic) for help. Ask for the obsession with alcohol, drugs, sugar, sex, or whatever to be removed. This doesn't mean you won't have sex ever again. It does mean that the sex you have won't land you in jail or a clinic to get treatment for a disease you can't spell.

Read the literature of your Twelve Step fellowship. Some people say the easiest way to hide a $100 bill from an alcoholic is to stick it in his Big Book. Whatever fellowship you're in, read that fellowship's Big Book or Basic Text, the AA Big Book (it set the tone for all the others), or both. Learn all you can about addiction and recovery. The material is just sitting there in a pile or on racks in the meeting room. Grab some. It's free.

Get meeting lists, which provide the names, phone numbers, and often email addresses of the members of each group. Even call random people on the list. They will be surprisingly happy to hear from you. It's free.

Work the Twelve Step slogans:

"Turn it over": whatever you're going through—and ask your Higher Power for help.

"Think": don't just operate on automatic pilot.

"First things first": do what you need to do, and only then do what you want to do. Pay your bills if you can. Get a job or keep the job you have.

"Live and let live": quit trying to control everyone around you, and go enjoy your own life. It's amazing how much more time and money you'll have now that you're clean.

"But for the grace of God": just think of where your life would be if you hadn't cleaned up.

"Just for today": you can drink and use all you want tomorrow. I have a friend who often says in meetings, "I'll be getting drunk at 12:01 a.m.," and then he names the bar where you can find him. Of course, since AA is a day-at-a-time program, we only have to not drink (or not drug or not whatever) just for these twenty-four hours.

Once it's 12:01 a.m., it's a new day, so he won't drink that day, either.

And above all, **"Easy does it"** . . . but do it! The old-timers suggest we wear our program like a loose garment and not allow the halo to slip down from over our heads and choke us.

If need be, take things one breath at a time. The *decision* to stop using or drinking is a solitary one. It's just something we all do, like being born, or dying.

Narcotics Anonymous will have its own specific suggestions about how to stop taking drugs. The same is true of Marijuana Anonymous, and so on. The program supports you when you've made the decision to stop drinking, using, or continuing any of the behaviors you know have been keeping you from living your best life. Twelve Step programs help you face and make the changes that *you* need in *your* life. ■

Q. Once You've *Stopped,* How Do You *Stay Stopped*?

A. In other words, how do you continue to reinforce the decision you've made to give up alcohol or other drugs? It's not easy; if it were easy, nobody would ever drink or use again. And yet, you often hear people talking in meetings about having "relapsed," or about approaches that provide "relapse prevention."

I don't like the word *relapse,* because there's a certain passivity to the term. A person could have cancer, get chemo, and through no fault of his or her own, the cancer can reoccur. It's often just bad luck. That's relapse. With drinking and using, however, relapse is not a passive experience. The same way we decide to quit drinking and using, we actually make a decision to start up again. There may be a lag of hours or even days from the time we decide to start again until the moment we actually pick up, but it's a conscious decision that most of us can look back on—a moment when we gave ourselves permission to drink and use again. We actively decide to slip.

So don't come 'round here with that relapse talk; I don't buy it. Or as my sponsor says, alcoholics and addicts don't taper off. We taper on.

And here you are, deciding not to drink or use again, and that's great. So how do you stay stopped? The easiest way to answer this question is to step back and recognize that we have a disease called alcoholism or addiction. So let's see what those terms really mean, because once we have a clearer understanding of addiction and alcoholism, it's easier to stay stopped.

To try to understand how Twelve Step recovery programs think about addiction and alcoholism, let's go back to how Alcoholics Anonymous, the first program, defines alcoholism. AA sees alcoholism as a threefold disease. It's physical—there's a physical compulsion to keep drinking long after the sane person would stop. It's mental—there's a mental obsession with alcohol, a sense that you can trust alcohol in a way that you cannot trust anyone or anything else. Once you get the physical compulsion and the mental obsession, then you end up with what Alcoholics Anonymous calls a spiritual loss of values. These thoughts are applicable to any form of addiction or behavior that you think might have started directing itself.

We all know what values are. We acquire them at home, from our parents, older siblings, teachers, coaches, religious leaders, or other older and presumably wiser people. Alcohol is called the "great eraser" because it wipes out all those decent values we had and replaces them with a single value—killing pain.

If you ask me why most alcoholics and addicts drink and use, I would say the simple answer is to kill pain. We have emotional pain, and we don't want to feel it. Addicts and alcoholics are sensitive people in an abrasive world, and we need something to take the edge off. That's why we drink and get high. I'm sure there are more complicated reasons, but I'm not smart enough to understand them.

The Big Book speaks of an "allergy" to alcohol—and the possession of this allergy is what makes alcoholics vitally different from other people. Interestingly, Joe and Charlie were two alcoholics who toured the country with a presentation called "The Big Book Comes Alive."[1] Joe and Charlie disputed this point. They said that alcoholics actually *lack* an allergy to alcohol. Let's put this in clearer terms. Ever got stung by a bee? Do you have a sudden desire to find a beehive and put your hand in it? That's because your body has a naturally occurring allergy to bee stings. Once you've been stung once, you will do anything in your power not to get stung again. That's the power of an allergy.

By contrast, when an alcoholic or addict has one drink, or one hit, or one bump, or one whatever, he or she says, "I want more."

Which is to say, according to Joe and Charlie, that *everyone else* has an allergy to alcohol, except for alcoholics, who keep drinking until they "feel no pain"—and then keep drinking some more.

I once heard a guy in a meeting say, "If there were somebody who came up to me and said, 'I've got a pill that you could take that would solve all your problems,' I would respond, 'I'll take two.'"

This is a long way of saying that at heart, alcoholism is a spiritual malady or illness. The American Medical Association has long acknowledged that alcoholism is a disease, so you don't have to just take AA's word for that point. What kind of disease do we understand alcoholism to be? A physical compulsion, coupled with a mental obsession, leading to a spiritual loss of values.

Let's move from the specific case of alcoholism to the general issue of addiction. My understanding is that a person is addicted to a substance or activity if, when one desires to stop, the person is unable to stop.

I've heard debates about whether you can really be addicted to food or even cigarettes. My understanding is that people—and I'm one of them—can use sugar in an addictive manner.

Others say that overeating is a habituation instead of an addiction.

Same thing with smoking.

To me, these are distinctions without differences. If you can't stop when you want to stop, and if you can't stay stopped, chances are you're dealing with addiction. And if you are, you might as well get clean. ▪

A. Here's where things get interesting: The insurance policy against drinking or using again, the thing that stands between you and the next drink or drug, is not a purely intellectual solution. It's not a mantra that you can repeat over and over. It's not a solution of mind over matter.

It's a spiritual solution.

The great psychologist and AA benefactor Carl Jung said that the use of alcohol is a low-level quest for God. Remember, AA is the blueprint for all other Twelve Step programs. So, let's go back to that blueprint for a second and try to figure out how and why it applies to addiction in general. The Twelve Steps constitute a higher-level quest for God, one that won't get you arrested or locked up, one that won't hurt your liver or put you in a position to overdose, destroy your marriage, or otherwise ruin your day.

So what exactly is the purpose of the Twelve Steps?

A hint can be found in the way old-timers sometimes read the Twelve Steps when called upon to do so in meetings. When they get to the Twelfth Step, they take the word *the* and give it a little extra oomph. As in, "Having had a spiritual awakening as *the* result of these steps . . ."

In other words, they are implying that if you take the first eleven Steps, your spirit will reawaken. Why do you need a spiritual awakening? Because it's only when our spirit is asleep that we feel the need to further anesthetize it with alcohol, drugs, or other substances and behaviors. We have a God-sized hole inside of us, and we would seek to fill it with substances and activities that distract us from the emotional pain we wish we didn't have to feel. When your spirit is reawakened, the pain diminishes. Life becomes livable. A lot of it vanishes over time as we become better, more successful, and more humble people.

I was once at a meeting where you could ask questions of the speaker after he gave a twenty-minute pitch. One speaker had twenty-five years. I asked him how he went from where he was to where he is now.

"It's a four-letter word: P-A-I-N. Pain. I processed the pain."

The Steps are a proven means of processing the pain that leads us alcoholics and addicts to drink or use—that includes pain of which we are not consciously aware. By processing the pain, we *feel* better and so we *get* better—without the urge to drink or use. On top of that, we stop making other things in our lives generally worse. When we stop our addictive behavior, we eventually stop doing the things that create feelings of shame. We stop hurting and using other people and therefore hurting ourselves. We stop getting fired. We stop destroying relationships and families, and people usually stop breaking up with us.

Okay, it's not as though you get sober and you never lose another relationship. But water finds its own level—we are only attracted to (and attractive to) people at our own spiritual level in life. As we get physically, mentally, and spiritually fit, we tend to choose healthier people, and relationships usually go better. Does every sober relationship work out? No, and, well, that's life. If things don't work out, we are able to act with dignity instead of embarrassment and misery, which is the hallmark of the practicing alcoholic or addict.

It takes time and tools—most powerfully the Steps—to process the pain, to awaken a spirit that has been dormant for years or even decades.

The purpose of the first eleven Steps, then, is to reawaken the spirit of the alcoholic or addict so that he or she no longer feels the compulsion to drink or use. (What's the Twelfth Step for, you ask? We'll get there.)

Does this mean that your life suddenly gets great? Quite the contrary. Clancy I., a legendary figure in the program in Southern California and one of my grand-sponsors, says it best. According to Clancy, if you stop drinking and using and all of your problems go away, you probably aren't an alcoholic or addict. But if you stop drinking and using and then everything piles up on you, there's a good chance that you're "one of us." ■

Q. What Do the Twelve Steps Do, and Why Are There Twelve of Them, Anyway?

A. We talked in the previous section about how the overall purpose of the Steps is to create the spiritual awakening—the re-awakening of the spirit—that makes it possible for an alcoholic or addict to live without alcohol or other drugs.

Again, when you go to meetings, you get the idea that everybody knows what the Steps do, how they work, and why they are in the order in which they're presented. In reality, today, you could go to a lot of meetings and never hear a word about the Steps. Sad but true. The Steps might be posted on the wall. Somebody might read the Steps out loud at the beginning of the meeting. The meeting may even be billed as a "Step Study" in which the topic is supposed to be . . . you guessed it . . . the Steps.

But the reality is often otherwise. Even in meetings supposedly dedicated to the discussion of the Steps, people sometimes put their hands up and talk about whatever they feel like—something going on in their lives, a job they're trying to get, a significant other who is giving them a hard time. (What do you call a male alcoholic or addict without a girlfriend? Homeless.) Or, as I've mentioned before, there's my personal favorite: how a person's cat is doing.

Talk about the well-being of a cat is not going to help me get sober. If there were one thing I would change about Twelve Step meetings,* it would be that no one would be allowed to discuss cats at any time, even if the cat got drunk or high.

---

*Okay, you've seen that line before in this book. Guess what—you'll hear it again.

I mentioned at the outset that we are living in a post-spiritual era of Twelve Step programs, which is a grave shame. If we aren't living the Steps, which constitute the path to spirituality in recovery, then what are we? We're in trouble, that's what we are. So since it's possible to go to tons of meetings and hear nothing about the Steps, let's spend some time now and get a sense of how they fit together.

The first three Steps are about acknowledging the problem of addiction or alcoholism and accepting spiritual help. Through Step One we acknowledge that we cannot drink or use in safety. Step Two brings us to acknowledge that some sort of help is available. Step Three moves us to agree to accept that help.

As Bill W. wrote, the first two Steps are yes-or-no, up-or-down decisions. You don't have to do any writing. You don't have to fill out forms. All you have to do is agree or disagree. If you agree that you've got a drinking or drug problem, or a debting or a sex or a food problem, or what would be considered a people problem in Al-Anon, then you've taken Step One.

If you believe that something can help you, whether it's a traditional belief in God, a nontraditional belief in a Higher Power, or even the fellowship itself (it's said that G-O-D stands for "group of drunks"), you've taken Step Two.

No fuss, no muss. It's a yes-or-no decision. Either you think something can help you or you don't. Once you do, perhaps because you've been inspired by all those people in all those meetings who claim that something helped them, you've taken Step Two.

Step Three is a bit more complicated, but not much more complicated. It just means that you're willing to allow the Power you noticed in Step Two to help you with the addiction problem you acknowledged in Step One. There's more to it, of course, but for now, Step Three is simply a decision to let that Power help you with your problem, nothing more.

Okay, those are the first three Steps.

Then come the next four. Step Four is the inventory Step, which everyone is so terrified about. The founders of Alcoholics Anonymous never intended that Step Four would become the exercise in voluminous autobiography into which it has morphed over the years.

The Big Book uses the phrase "grosser handicaps"—in other words, what are the main negative behaviors or bad habits that the alcoholic or addict possesses that he or she might like to be rid of? Why do we do this? As you've seen, the point of the Steps is to have a spiritual awakening, which means to deepen one's relationship with one's Higher Power to the point where we no longer find it necessary to drink or use.

Certain behaviors stand in the way of living a spiritual life. It's tough to be spiritual when you're angry, full of self-pity, resentful, impatient, projecting (you're thinking about the future, usually in negative terms), manipulating people, procrastinating, and so on.

The Fourth Step simply asks us to acknowledge these "grosser handicaps"—it doesn't ask us to write the history of every stupid thing we did from fourth grade to the present. As Joe and Charlie of "The Big Book Comes Alive" fame put it, 95 percent of the things people write down in these lengthy Fourth Steps have nothing to do with their alcoholism or addiction.

Everybody's afraid of doing a Fourth Step, but everybody has pretty much the same list of defects of character, which my sponsor calls bad habits—the aforementioned anger, fear, procrastination, manipulation, self-pity, resentment, projection, and so on. As Elvis Costello sang years ago, "There's no such thing as an original sin." This is why Twelve Step programs work so well—we are interchangeable under the skin.

It's not as though addicts and alcoholics are the only people in the world who have these negative traits. The difference is that when *we* get into these modes of being, when *we* get angry, self-pitying, resentful, and so on, we react by going out and using or drinking a case of beer, and then getting behind the wheel of a car.

Nonalcoholics and people who aren't addicts don't do that.

I don't know what they do, but they don't get loaded and look for their car keys.

So the Fourth Step asks us to identify those behaviors. Interestingly, it's those very behaviors—the anger and the self-pity and the fear and the resentment—*that kept us alive when we were drinking or using.* When I was out there, I did not want to let you get to know me, because if you did, you would hate me as much as I hated me. You would reject me as much as I rejected myself.

So all those behavioral traits—anger, fear, and so on—were the means by which I distanced myself from you, because if I could hide who I was, I had a better chance of getting from you whatever I needed—friendship, sex, companionship, shelter, whatever—than if you knew who I really was.

Now that we're no longer playing that dismal game, we don't have to rely on those bad habits. Instead, we recognize that they are now obstacles to the spiritual life we are seeking to lead.

Let me take a moment to unpack what I mean when I refer to *spiritual life.* People often carry a lot of baggage around when it comes to the word *spiritual.* Here's what I don't mean, and what the program doesn't mean when it comes to being spiritual. I don't mean perfection. I don't mean going off to a seminary or monastery or special place and living angelic lives. I don't mean sitting for hours a day in a special position chanting a mantra that will miraculously fix everything. Those things are all great, but that's not the context here. What I *do* mean is that we finally get to do the things that normal people do, without totally screwing up—having a relationship, holding a job, building a family, earning and (think of it!) saving money.

Some people say a balanced alcoholic or addict is one with a chip on both shoulders; I'm talking about the program helping us learn to live with *real* balance. So when I refer to the spiritual life, I mean living decently, like the guy across the street, the guy you can't understand because he's pretty much always in a decent mood, and when he rolls his recycle bin out to the street on Wednesday mornings, it isn't clinking with empty beer or wine bottles, like yours.

So the Fourth Step is just a list. Interestingly, back in the day, when AA started, it only took about half an hour to write a Fourth Step. And guess who did the writing? Not the newcomer, whose hand was often shaking too much, along with the rest of his body, from the alcohol. Yes, people did the Steps immediately after getting sober back then, which is why AA had a self-described success rate of 50 to 75 percent. In other words, half to three-quarters of the people who relied on AA as a program and started taking the Steps quickly got and stayed sober.

What's the rate today? Three percent? Two percent?

I don't know how you measure it, but I know I sure see a lot of newcomers in their first few days or weeks, and not that many are staying sober for a year or more. Twelve Step programs work great, but we members are doing a poor job of sharing the program with newcomers. They are paying for our ignorance, and they are often paying with their lives.

Getting back to Step Four, back in the day, the old-timer would do the writing of the inventory, not the newcomer. It would be done in thirty minutes. I have a photocopy of a Fourth Step from 1950. It's simply a handwritten list of "character defects"—the bad habits we enumerated moments ago, with checkmarks next to the ones with which the new member identified. No fuss, no muss. No autobiography. And no getting drunk in between the Third and Fourth Steps. That's how Twelve Step recovery should be.

Then comes Step Five, the act of sharing with our Higher Power and with another member of the program the results of our Fourth Step. If you wrote your inventory with another member of the program, you've already taken care of some of that sharing. Maybe now you can see why, back then, people used to take their Steps pretty quickly.

The old-timer would then ask the newcomer something like this: "Would you be willing to give up these character defects just for the day?" That question is the heart of the Sixth Step.

To which the newcomer would likely say yes, and before you know it you are on to the Seventh Step.

If the newcomer said no, the sponsor would cagily ask, "Would you be willing to be willing?" Or even, "Would you be willing to be willing to be willing?"

On some level, pretty much every human being would rather live a life without all that anger, fear, self-pity, and the rest of those negative traits. If—on any level—the person going through the Steps is able to acknowledge the desire to be rid of those things, he or she has taken Step Six.

In doing Step Seven we ask the Higher Power of our understanding to remove those character defects from us, in whatever manner and at whatever speed the Higher Power feels appropriate. As part of the Step, there's a prayer that Bill W. wrote that's found on page 76 of the current, fourth edition of the Big Book, called the Seventh Step Prayer; sometimes the sponsor and the sponsee will say that prayer together.

In addition to saying the Seventh Step Prayer, we try to practice the opposite of traits that have become all too familiar in our lives. For example, instead of anger, we try to be patient. Instead of manipulation, we try to practice "Live and let live." Instead of fear, we try to practice faith. Instead of self-pity, we try to practice gratitude. In so doing, we gradually leave behind, with the help of our Higher Power, the state of "obstinacy, sensitiveness, and unreasoning prejudice," as the Big Book puts it. We move into a state of reasonableness and, dare I say it, *spiritual living.*

So far, the first seven Steps have taken place within the walls of one's Twelve Step program. All of that changes with the Eighth Step, in which we make a list of people we have harmed and we get ready to apologize to them. *Amend* means to fix. We are trying to fix broken relationships. We are removing another stumbling block between ourselves and our Higher Power—the guilt we feel over the unfortunate things we might have done while we were out there drinking and using.

So with this Step, we make a list and check our list with our sponsor to make sure we have *actually harmed* the people on the list. Alcoholics and addicts sometimes love to grovel in front of other people, just so that we can be told that we weren't that bad. This Step is not about an opportunity to humiliate ourselves. It's a chance to set things right as best we can with the people we've harmed. If a reality check with a sponsor hints that something on the list doesn't really boil down to harm, then the list gets shortened.

My list included ex-girlfriends, ex-employers, and so on. No ex-employer offered to hire me back. I did get a nice note from a former boss, himself a recovering alcoholic, who "got it." But he certainly did not offer to rehire me. Of the ex-girlfriends, most seemed happy for me but certainly wanted nothing further to do with me—once burned, twice shy. One did ask me out again; some people never learn.

The goal is to right old wrongs as best we can. One's sponsor typically has guidance about how to approach people to whom we are making amends. We don't have to tell them that we're in AA or NA or any A. We don't point out *their* behavior—it's not comparative negligence.

We're just apologizing for what we did wrong; "Cleaning up our side of the street" is the common Twelve Step phrase.

We also don't use the amends process to reignite old arguments. We also don't make apologies for things that could conceivably make things worse for the other person—that's an important thing to keep in mind. We don't have to apologize to our drug dealer—we never harmed him, even if we didn't pay that one time. He made a fine living that year anyway. So by the time we get to Step Nine and we're actually making the amends, we have moved from the safety and security of our Twelve Step program into the real world, where we must live.

It's not healthy to hide out in meetings for the rest of your life and just talk a good, spiritual game. The Big Book says, "The spiritual life is not a theory. *We have to live it.*" Hiding out in a program is, as I once heard in a meeting, like "eating the menu." It's not enough.

Sometimes we write letters to people who no longer can be found, although thanks to Facebook and other social media, it's easier and easier to find the people we hurt. We write letters to people who've passed away and read them to our sponsors or at the graveside. And we write letters to ourselves apologizing for the way we treated ourselves.

My sponsor makes a big deal about the fact that alcoholics and addicts have been putting themselves at the top of the list for far too long. He does not believe that we should put ourselves at the top of our Eighth Step amend list. I agree. (I have to, because he will read this book.) I recall that when I made my amend to myself, my sponsor had me write a letter to myself, which he had me read to him over the phone. I began reading, "Dear Me, I'm sorry for what I did to myself." He stopped me and told me, "Read it again, but this time say your name and say 'you' instead of what you were reading."

I shrugged and did what he said.

"Dear Michael, I'm sorry I treated you so badly. I'm sorry I acted as if I didn't love you"—or words to that effect—and I broke into tears.

You can see that this whole process, from the first three Steps where we accept spiritual help, to the next four Steps where we get to know ourselves a little better, and the next two Steps where we identify the wrongs we did and try to make them right, taken together, increase the likelihood that we are going to have a shot at a spiritual life. Again, if the phrase *spiritual life* still doesn't resonate with you, you can think about what a nonspiritual life is, and how you get to avoid that.

The *nonspiritual* life is one in which we use people, get fired a lot, get thrown out of places, embarrass ourselves and others, have a hard time looking people in the eye, and are generally depressed and miserable most of the time. If this is a nonspiritual life, and it is, think of the spiritual life as simply the opposite of all those things.

At Step Ten, we are asked to continue to monitor our behavior and make amends "when" we are wrong as opposed to "if" we are wrong. In other words, we're going to be wrong from time to time, just as we've been in the past. We're going to say the wrong thing. We're going to do the wrong thing. These things happen in life—even when you are working a program. As the Big Book says, "We are not saints." We are human beings, trying to live life on different terms, fumbling with this new set of tools we are acquiring, and not necessarily doing things perfectly.

Perfectionism, by the way, is a common trait of addicts and alcoholics. We try to be perfect because we want to avoid criticism. The only problem with perfectionism as a strategy for avoiding criticism is that the very people who criticize us are too imperfect themselves to notice how perfect we are. So it doesn't work.

Step Ten recognizes that we will continue to make mistakes from time to time, so we simply apologize rather than say things like, "He had it coming," or, "I was doing the best I could," or other such excuses and obfuscations. My favorite of these, of course, is what they say in the South: "He needed killing."

Step Eleven asks us to pray and meditate. Now that we've come so far, cleaning out the obstacles to our relationship with our Higher Power, we want to go more deeply into that relationship. Interestingly, today we think of prayer and meditation in Step Eleven as two separate if somewhat related activities.

Back in the day, when the program was founded, "prayer and meditation" were seen as one activity—prayer was where you talked to God, and meditation was where you got quiet and listened to see what God had to say.

The whole concept of meditation as silencing the mind—the Transcendental Meditation or Eastern approach—wasn't really popular in the West until the 1970s. When the program was founded in the 1930s, *meditation* didn't mean sitting on the floor with your legs crossed and your index fingers and thumbs forming perfect letter Os.

Prayer and meditation back then really meant, in our terms, prayer and contemplation. So if you don't like to sit still for very long and focus on your breathing, good news—that's not how the old boys did it when they set this whole thing up. But that's a story for another day.

Finally, if we did everything we were asked in the first eleven Steps, spirits reawaken. Again, the phrase is, "Having had a spiritual awakening as *the* result of these steps. . . ." A reawakened spirit doesn't need to drink. Life is good. The payoff is Step Twelve. We try to carry this message to alcoholics and addicts, because we cannot keep the program unless we share it with others. And we try to "practice these principles in all our affairs"—meaning that we don't just act like we are living a good program when we're at meetings. We actually try to act like decent citizens wherever we go. As my sponsor says, "If you act like a decent person, and you talk like a decent person, and you work like a decent person, eventually people will start mistaking you for a decent person."

So there you have it. A brief summary of how the Steps work and why we have twelve of them. Later, we'll talk more about who and what influenced the Steps. Right now, you might feel that the Steps are overly complicated. You're not alone. But that doesn't mean they don't help. Keep reading. ■

A. Yes, it does sound complicated.

Maybe even too complicated. Dr. Bob, the Akron-based physician who became the second member of Alcoholics Anonymous, thought Bill's Twelve Steps were overly complicated, and he didn't like them. In fact, he liked them so little that he wrote his own AA literature, which had a four-step program, not a Twelve Step program. The first step was the equivalent of Bill's first three Steps—acknowledging the problem and the solution, and accepting spiritual help. Bob called that *Conversion*.

The next four steps—our Steps Four through Seven—Bob boiled down to his second step, which he called *Introspection*.

Steps Eight and Nine, the amends Steps, became a single step three in Bob's formulation—*Restitution*.

Steps Ten, Eleven, and Twelve became Bob's step four—*Witness*, in which you carried the message to others or "witnessed," in early twentieth-century spiritual language, to others about what you had gained in AA.

In Bill's first draft of the Steps, there were only six. He just kept adding until he got to twelve.

I'm not pointing all of this out to cause confusion about the program, or to tear down the value of Twelve Step recovery. Quite the opposite. I mention it to highlight that it is not necessary to get caught up in the wording, or who did what. It's the *actions* and *intentions* that matter. So whether you like Bob's four steps or Bill's twelve, it doesn't matter. What matters is that you take the actions. Too frequently, newcomers are given the impression that simply by going to enough meetings and counting days, they will scramble to safety and never have to drink or use again. It's just not how it works.

Go to enough meetings, and you'll hear about people who had ten, twenty, or thirty years of sobriety, or even longer, who started drinking or using again. Why? It's the same old story. They got away from meetings. They got away from the fellowship. They got away from the Steps. And sure enough, it doesn't matter how much time you have—if you stop doing these things, you will pick up. A friend of mine says that he's one hundred beers from the penitentiary. He's right—if not about himself, then certainly about me.

Alcoholism and addiction are progressive, which means that the disease gets worse as time goes on—*even if you're not drinking or using.* This means that if you would pick up after five years sober, you wouldn't be resuming the drinking or using habits that you had five years earlier. You would be drinking or using now as if you'd been doing so for the past five years.

That's certainly not something I would like to experience, or inflict upon my loved ones, and I'm sure you feel the same way. We say that as long as you stick to the basics, you'll never have to go back to basics. As long as you start your day on your knees asking for help, life will never drive you to your knees. We have so many wonderful clichés—somebody ought to write a book.*

So now, like the salty old-timers sitting in the back of the room, the ones you have to touch to make sure they're actually still breathing and they haven't passed away during the meeting,

---

*Just call me "Someone." It's better than what my sponsor used to call me, which is "Some." As in "Some are sicker than others." He also said I could turn my will and my life over to the care of any empty room and get better results. He also said that I may not have had a happy childhood, but I sure am having a long one. What a mean sponsor I have.

if somebody asks you how the Steps work, instead of giving him a whole lecture based on this section of the book, you can just give a condescending smile and say, "They work just fine." ▪

Q. What Is Secret Step Zero?

A. I had no idea you knew about Step Zero! You're definitely a unique and special addict or alcoholic! So you've heard of Secret Step Zero, have you? It's like knowing the secret coffee options at Starbucks, or the secret menu at In-N-Out Burger, if you live on the West Coast.

Step Zero is as follows: "I'm tired of this s&%*!"

Before people take the Steps, they have to be tired of the way they're living. It takes effort, desire, focus, and the ability to look at oneself in a serious and sometimes critical manner. These are four things that most alcoholics and addicts would rather die than do. How do I know this is true? Most in fact do die rather than do these things.

The simple question is this: *Have you had enough?*

It's up to you to determine what *enough* is. You don't have to be homeless, pushing a shopping cart, living under a bridge, or some variant to decide that you've had enough misery. Maybe you've just lost enough—enough relationships, enough jobs, enough money, enough self-respect. It's really your call. No one else can decide that it's time for you to start your recovery—only you.

Other people may have opinions, and they may choose to express those opinions forcefully to you. Those people might include spouses, children, parents, law enforcement, and judges. But at the end of the day, it's your decision, not theirs. So if you're "tired of this s&%*!" that's good. It means that you've taken Secret Step Zero. And that means that you're ready to start taking the Steps.

Q. How Do I Actually Take the Steps?

A. The language of the Steps is complicated—perhaps overly complicated. Listening to people discuss them can be like listening to American history scholars debating the precise meaning of the Bill of Rights.

That's why it's helpful to find someone in the program to sponsor you and guide you through the Steps. They were written in such a manner that they are impossible to do all by oneself. So we choose mentors, whom we call sponsors, to take us through the Steps.

By the by, the reason we use the term *sponsor* when we really mean *mentor* goes back to the early days of AA, from around the time of its founding, in Akron, Ohio. Back then, one of the sources of potential new members for the then-unnamed fellowship was Akron City Hospital, where Dr. Bob practiced medicine. Hospital staff would identify for Dr. Bob patients who had been brought in for chronic alcoholism, and then Dr. Bob would "sponsor" or oversee their movement from the hospital's general population to a private room.

This would facilitate the visits of sober members of Alcoholics Anonymous, who would talk about their own troubles with booze and describe the spiritual solution that helped them stop and stay stopped. Strictly speaking, sponsorship meant getting a drunk a private hospital room, not mentoring him in the Steps. Time passed, and the word *sponsor* stuck.

As a result, we don't look for mentors—we look for sponsors. So how do you select a sponsor? There's really one simple test—the person "has something you want." The formulation is deliberately vague, so as to accommodate pretty much anyone who comes to Twelve Step recovery. Maybe the person has a nice car. Or a really solid career. Maybe that's what you want. Or maybe the person emanates a calmness, a sense of poise, that you wish you had. Or has a hot boyfriend or girlfriend. It doesn't matter as long as whatever that person has is something you perceive as a step up from whatever you have or don't have right now.

The idea is that if you go to enough meetings with people who are also working and living a program, you will find someone who has that special something *you want* and who will help you get that same thing for yourself—whether it is material, emotional, spiritual, or something else altogether.

It's deceptively brilliant. Some meetings assign sponsors, but for the most part, the choice is left to the newcomer. We say that "We have a wrench for every nut," which refers not just to meetings that will be appropriate and conducive for one person's recovery but not necessarily for another's, but also to mentor figures. The person you choose might be someone I wouldn't relate to. Somehow it all sorts itself out.

There are pitfalls, of course. When you ask someone to sponsor you, that person may say no.

We're not supposed to say no—we're supposed to say yes to every Twelve Step fellowship request. But not everybody plays by all the rules, all the time. There was one moment in my recovery around the time my first child was born that I felt so overwhelmed that I had to tell my sponsees I just couldn't continue. I resumed with some later, and some just moved on, which is fine. But by and large, whenever anyone has asked me, I've always said yes.

It may not work out with the first or even second person you pick. Remember that we are a nonprofessional organization and anyone with the desire to stop drinking or using can join any relevant Twelve Step program. As noted earlier, we are not saints. Some people in Twelve Step programs just don't have great people skills. Or they talk a good game in the meetings, but when you get them one on one, the results are disappointing.

It can happen that the first person you ask becomes your sponsor for life, but it's more likely that you will move from one to another over the course of time. I've had four AA sponsors through my first twenty-five years of sobriety. One has since passed away, and I am in regular contact with the other three, including the person who is my sponsor today. I cherish these relationships, as will you, I hope.

We addicts and alcoholics don't always know a lot about love. Some of us think we know a lot about sex, but frequently we don't know all that much about how to *relate lovingly* to another human being and have a relationship be successful. We know how to manipulate people through giving them the appearance of love, but when it comes to love itself, we come up short.

That's the case until we enter into a sponsorship relationship. This is really the first time that many of us have experienced, understood, and accepted unconditional love. In Twelve Step programs, everyone is rooting for everyone else. It's not like golf, where someone likes every shot. Nobody wants to see a fellow member of AA or NA or any A get drunk or high. We all want to see the other guy succeed.

This is one of the things that makes Twelve Step programs so special. The person you choose as your sponsor will most likely be honored that you've asked, and, I hope, will say yes. The act of sharing the program, which has saved our lives, with another human being desperate for the same kind of relief, is one of the most amazing things one human being can do for another. These are absolutely treasured relationships, and we do it for fun and for free. There are no dues or fees. We don't pay our sponsors for their time. Instead, we pay it forward. We turn around and help the next person. That's how the whole thing works.

The same thing holds true with the people we sponsor. I've had the privilege of sponsoring many, many men in AA, Al-Anon, and Debtors Anonymous. A few of those relationships have gone on for more than fifteen years. I love the men I've sponsored, and I love the fact that I can express love to others. Alas, at least three of my sponsees have died from alcohol and drug abuse; another committed suicide. Loss is part of the sponsorship experience. I don't regret going through those losses, although of course I wish these folks had stuck with the program and survived.

Maybe if you want, at the very end of the book, I'll tell you the story of my sponsee Kevin. It sums up why I'm so ardent about the program. Okay. But no peeking ahead to Kevin's story. Deal?

We've talked about the sponsor's role and why the sponsor is so important in the process of taking the Steps. Now let's get back to the Steps. There are variations on doing the Steps, both of which have dance terminology attached. There's two-stepping, which consists of taking Step One and Step Twelve and ignoring the intervening Steps. The idea here is that you acknowledge that you're powerless over drugs or alcohol, and then you become a re-nowned "circuit speaker," beloved to all and famous for carrying a fabulous message. The only problem is that you never got well by taking those other ten necessary Steps. So two-stepping is not really an effective shortcut.

There's also the three-step waltz, which consists of taking Steps One, Two, and Three over and over again—one-two-three, one-two-three, one-two-three. You're not exactly waltzing your way to a better life, though. We do have nine more Steps for you. It's terrific to acknowledge your alcoholism or addiction in the First Step, and acknowledge the fact that help exists in the Second Step, and accept the help in the Third, but why stop there? Unfortunately, many people do. They never get the full benefits of the recovery program, and their lives never develop as they might have hoped. Neither two-stepping nor the three-step waltz are recommended. That's why having a sponsor is vital— your sponsor will "recommend" that you get Step Four and the rest of the Steps done. Otherwise, if we sponsor ourselves, we're headed for trouble.

It's also suggested to take the Steps in order. You don't go out and make amends until you've done the earlier Steps. You don't go out and do a Fourth Step until you've already accepted the spiritual help available in the first three Steps. Addicts and alcoholics like to shake their fists and rebel against everything under the sun. In this case, the wiser course might be to acknowledge that maybe those people who go to the meetings and are sober might know something, and then do the program the way they suggest.

For a long time, I lived in Southern California, and I've been to a lot of meetings in that area. As a friend of mine in Santa Monica meetings says, "I went to the dumb meetings. I listened to the dumb people. I read the dumb book. I took the dumb Steps. And I got really, really smart." ■

Q. So, How Did *You* Pick *Your* Sponsor?

A. Six years before I got sober, I had yet another fight with yet another girlfriend. It was probably over the fact that she accused me of being a liar.

Why did she do that?

Maybe . . . because I was a liar. Survey says?

She'd asked me if I'd gone out that morning in the car, and I said no. I had.

"Then why was the radio on when I got into the car just now?" she asked, perplexed. "It wasn't on last night."

And one thing led to another, and she accused me of lying. Which hurt my feelings.

So I went and took a bath.

Why I took a bath, I have no idea. But while I lay there in the bathtub, I heard a voice. It cut through my misery and gloom and said, "I love you, and I will never leave you."

I looked around the bathroom. Who said that? Was the radio on?

No one else. No radio. Just me. Lying in a bathtub, feeling a lot of self-pity because my girlfriend had (accurately) accused me of being a liar and we had fought over it.

And here I am hearing voices.

Cut to, as they say in the movie industry, six years later. I'm living in Los Angeles and I've decided I'm an alcoholic and must now choose an AA sponsor. So I tell myself I'll go to the noon meeting, which at the time was held at the Sizzler restaurant, at

Bundy and Wilshire. I let my Higher Power lead me to the right choice in His (or her or its) inscrutable way.

The format of the meeting was that the leader would point to men one at a time and they would share for a few minutes.

I listened carefully to each speaker, waiting for some sort of sign from God as to which man I should choose to be my sponsor.

By halfway through the meeting, it felt like a fool's errand. Why on earth did I believe that God would send me a sign in an AA meeting about which sponsor I was to choose? Didn't God have bigger fish to fry?*

And then the leader called on an older gentleman named Hal. He had been an actor and spoke dramatically, with a deep Southern accent.

He told the story about a moment of deep depression prior to his sobriety.

"And then I heard a voice," he continued. "I didn't know where the voice was coming from. And the voice said, 'I love you, and I will never leave you.'"

As comedian Bill Engvall says, in a different context, "Here's your sign."

I asked Hal to be my sponsor and he agreed. His grand-sponsor was Bill Wilson himself, so I was drinking from the fire hose. Hal gave me an awesome foundation in AA, and as a result in Twelve Step programs, and I am passing along to you many of the things he taught me. ■

---

*Maybe the fact that the restaurant was called "Sizzler" was a sign that God did not have bigger fish to fry.

Q. What Is the Big Book, and Why Do I Have to Read Something from the 1930s?

A. Within two years of its founding, AA was miniscule by our standards—there might not have been fifty or sixty sober people in its ranks. You could only find meetings in Akron, Cleveland, and New York City, and in those places, meetings were seldom more often than once a week.

AA wasn't listed in the phone book. Al Gore had not yet invented the Internet, so you couldn't just search online to find a meeting. You had to be a very lucky alcoholic to find your way to AA back then. And yes, at the time, the only group was AA; there wasn't yet a program for addicts of other stripes. So the question arose: how do you spread the message to an even wider circle of drunks?

Bill Wilson, AA's cofounder, was a relentless promoter. He actually thought of naming AA the Bill W. Society, and it would offer a chain of for-profit hospitals to serve alcoholics across the country. Never one to think small, Bill saw moneymaking potential in AA practically from the start. Wiser heads prevailed, and fortunately, Twelve Step recovery has never been about the money.

But back to the late 1930s and the question of how to raise the visibility and membership of Alcoholics Anonymous. At that time, pretty much the only answer was to do a book. Bill actually started a publishing company, Works Publishing, as in, "Faith without works is dead," one of his favorite biblical quotes. He raised funds from a variety of sources, promising them a great return when the book explaining AA was published and became an instant moneymaker.

Of course, that's not what happened. There's a famous story in AA Bill liked to tell that when they launched the Big Book, their marketing campaign consisted of direct mail to doctors, whom they figured had ready access to large numbers of drunks. Included in the mailings about the Big Book, which has always carried the actual title *Alcoholics Anonymous,* was a penny postcard allowing doctors to request more information or buy copies.

Bill and his cohorts excitedly headed over to the post office near Grand Central Station with large sacks, so that he could carry back to their office all the orders that the doctors sent in. Of course, there were only about eleven orders, and some of them in handwriting so poor (doctors! Or maybe drunken doctors!) that they couldn't even figure out who the purchaser was.

The Big Book, in short, was a flop. The book languished until the *Saturday Evening Post,* the most popular magazine of its day, did what was intended as an investigative story on AA, exposing it for the fraud it surely was. Drunks getting sober? Just by sitting around in chairs and enlarging their spiritual lives? It had to be a racket.

The *Saturday Evening Post* assigned the story to an investigative reporter, Jack Alexander, who had just concluded an investigation into racketeering in Philadelphia. Magazine executives figured he was the perfect man to investigate the fraud that AA had to be.

Alexander spent considerable time with Bill, attending meetings and meeting other sober alcoholics. Instead of writing a hatchet job on AA, which was essentially what the magazine had commissioned, he wrote an article so praiseful of the fledgling fellowship that AA actually got the rights to republish it, and you can still find it online and in pamphlet form, available for free at meetings to this day.

Since the *Saturday Evening Post* was one of the most popular magazines in early 1940s America, suddenly the book took off. And so did the fellowship. Thousands upon thousands of people ordered the book, and for the first time in its young history, AA was rolling in dough and influence.

It was also rolling in newcomers, and it had to figure out how to assimilate all these potential new members. As Joe and Charlie said, "We were hooking them faster than we could string them."

AA also benefitted from an appearance by Bill Wilson on a popular national radio program—again, this was before TV or the Internet. A radio host named Gabriel Heatter had Bill come on the program. People trusted this Heatter chap, and between the *Saturday Evening Post* article and the radio appearance, AA was suddenly on the map.

And so was the Big Book.

So what exactly is the Big Book? What's in it and what's all the fuss about? Why was it so important to the explosive growth of Alcoholics Anonymous, and why is it still so important today?

The Big Book took its nickname from the Sears catalog, which was the equivalent of the Internet in home shopping back in the day. The idea of the book was to give people the experience of what Alcoholics Anonymous offered without the necessity of actually attending a meeting. Again, when it was written, you could only find meetings in three cities and two states. What if you lived far away? The Big Book was meant to fill that gap—to explain the recovery program for alcoholism to those who did not have the benefit of a meeting nearby.

Today, we live in an era where you can say virtually anything to anyone, or show virtually anything in a movie, cable TV show, book, or Internet video, and no one will blink an eye. Back then, you could not talk openly about alcoholism (or any other seemingly immoral activity). It just wasn't done. And yet, here came this book, courageously describing the merciless nature of the disease. No one had ever seen anything like it.

The book described, in graphic terms for its era, what alcoholism was, why it was a disease and not a moral issue, and how to tell if you were an alcoholic yourself. The book offered polite American society an impolite (yet honest) view of the disease, and also, equally important, a view of the recovery process. The book recognized from the start the challenges it faced—convincing alcoholics that they were alcoholic; helping them understand what the disease was; and then describing the spiritual nature of the solution, which is something that practically no newcomer wanted then (or wants today).

The book devotes more than fifty pages to creating a sense of identification between the reader and the author, which was mostly Bill with the Akron AA members looking over his shoulder, commenting and editing. Bill, it is said, wrote the book in longhand, on yellow legal pads, and had the pages typed by his longtime assistant, Nell Wing.

The book begins with "The Doctor's Opinion," written by William Silkworth, MD, the medic who ran Towns Hospital, where Bill went to dry out, and where Bill had a transcendent spiritual experience that meant he would never have to drink again (more on that later).

Remember that the initial appeal of the book was aimed at doctors; it was thought that having a doctor give his stamp of support at the beginning of the book would give its readers confidence that what the book offered was legitimate.

On a personal level, "The Doctor's Opinion" is one of my favorite things in all of recovery literature. In it, Silkworth wrote that readers can "rely" on anything the authors say about themselves, the disease, and the recovery program. It also described the "phenomenon of craving," which separates alcoholics and addicts from other people—the compulsion to keep on drinking and using long after the normal person would have said, "I'm starting to feel it," and pushed away the remainder of his or her drink.

"The Doctor's Opinion" also tells a story, which I particularly related to in my first year, about how an alcoholic had come to Dr. Silkworth, trembling and fearful. Dr. Silkworth sent him to AA, and the man returned some months later. Dr. Silkworth wrote that though he recognized the man's name, he barely recognized him, because he had been restored to health, sanity, and self-confidence.

I wanted to be that guy—someone who would be restored to life by the program, and thank you, God, I am.

Dr. Silkworth concluded, "I earnestly advise every alcoholic to read this book through, and though perhaps he came to scoff, he may remain to pray."

In chapter 1, Bill wrote his own story—his rise and fall, and further fall, and further fall, as an alcoholic. He recounted a visit from a former classmate, Ebby Thatcher, during which their conversation turned to the idea of choosing one's own concept of God.

This was a watershed moment in Bill's life. Like most people, he had gone to religious services as a child where he was told, "This is our concept of God, and it's gonna be your concept of God, too. And if it isn't, God's gonna be plenty angry."

But here came his buddy Ebby, who might have gone to the same church as Bill in their little Vermont village, with the amazing idea that you can *choose your own concept of a Higher Power.*

Bill was blown away by this idea, as are many people who attend a Twelve Step meeting and learn the same thing. It doesn't matter what your concept of God is. It just matters that you aren't it.

Bill ended up drunk again, and returned to Dr. Silkworth's drying-out hospital. This time, Bill prayed, "If there be a God, let him show himself!" The room filled with white light and Bill, blown away by the experience, never drank again. AA members refer to this episode, sometimes enviously, as Bill's "white light experience."

Then, a few months later, there occurred the great moment of the founding of Alcoholics Anonymous—that fateful day in Akron, Ohio, in May 1935.

As we have discussed, Bill had gone to Akron to oversee one side of a proxy fight—an early corporate takeover, and his side failed. He was stuck in Akron over a weekend with nothing to do. He paced the lobby of the hotel he was staying in, and his attention was—as to be expected—drawn to the hotel bar. Famously, he started dialing phone numbers to try to reach clergymen who might be able to put him in touch with a drunk to talk to. Eventually, that led to a fateful conversation with a Reverend Walter Tunks, who led him to the heiress Henrietta Sieberling, who led to the drunken proctologist Dr. Bob Smith.*

That's our unlikely history, and it is summarized in the opening pages of the Big Book.

From there, we learn that there is a spiritual solution to the disease we share. We also learn more about the disease and are presented with the purpose of the book: ". . . to enable you to find a Power greater than yourself which will solve your problem."

The problem, of course, being alcoholism.

What follows in the rest of the book? Well, the book then lists and describes the Twelve Steps and offers guidance as to how to take them. Fortunately or unfortunately, that guidance is open to plenty of interpretation. The fellowship had only been in existence for a couple of years when the book was written, and the Steps, as formally described in the Big Book, were essentially making their first appearance. So a lot of what's written about how the program works is really conjecture—it's how the program might work in Bill's perfect world. Some of what he wrote is exactly how things remain today.

---

*As the late, great Peppermint John—a legend in Southern California AA—used to say, this is proof that "AA has specialized in a**holes from the beginning."

Ultimately, there's more than one way to take the Steps. The main thing is that you do take them.

The publication of the Big Book was the first time where the Twelve Steps of Alcoholics Anonymous appeared in print. The fact that Bill varied the language in the Steps, using the phrases "defects of character," "shortcomings," and "wrongs" has been responsible for endless hours of pointless debate. Bill said that he never meant those words to be understood as different from each other. He just wanted to change the language so that the Steps didn't seem boring.

There's an entire chapter dedicated to working with others, the Twelfth Step, because of the supreme importance of carrying the message or paying it forward. Then comes a series of chapters on marriage, work, and family from which some great one-liners can be extracted—"We absolutely insist on enjoying life" and "But we aren't a glum lot" among them. But they aren't quite as polished or useful as the chapters that talk about the problem, the solution, and the Steps.

It's been said that Bill's wife, Lois, was extremely disappointed that Bill took it upon himself to write the chapter "To Wives"— she had wanted to write it. Lois's own frustrations with Bill, which did not diminish once he found sobriety, led her, in a fit of anger, to throw a shoe at him; that thrown shoe (history does not record whether it was a flat or a pump) led her to cofound the Al-Anon family groups, which provide Twelve Step recovery to family and friends of alcoholics.

The chapter "To Employers" is, well, a little flimsy if we're going to be honest. There's a certain amount of irony in the idea that an individual who had not held a real job in years, prior to his codeveloping AA, would write a chapter in which he pretended to be an employer talking to other employers. There's also a chapter called "The Family Afterward." The inclusion of this chapter is interesting when you consider that not too many years after Bill published the Big Book, he took up with a girlfriend and actually wrote her into his will, so that she would forever receive a percentage of his earnings on the Big Book.

When writing the final chapter, "A Vision for You," Bill was on firmer footing, describing the terror of late-stage alcoholism and the wonder of recovery. Many meetings conclude with the last paragraph or so from page 164, in which Bill wrote about trudging "the Road of Happy Destiny" and which gives us a final benediction, "May God bless you and keep you—until then." That same chapter gives us the wonderful image of "King Alcohol" and drunks as "shivering denizens" of King Alcohol's despotic reign.

So that's how the Big Book breaks down. From "The Doctor's Opinion" through chapter 6, pretty much everything rings true today. The language at times feels archaic, but most of the time, the book feels as though it were written an hour ago and not eighty years ago. Those three next-to-last chapters ("To Wives," "The Family Afterward," and "To Employers")? *Meh.* But the rest of the book stands the test of time.

The book, now in its fourth edition, also contains numerous individual stories of alcoholics who found their way to AA and recovered. With each additional edition, the editors have removed some stories and made way for others, to make the book more inclusive and to help more alcoholics and now addicts find a sense of identification. The stories also are often studied in Twelve Step meetings.

As the blueprint for all the Twelve Step programs, AA's Big Book gives you a primer on how a program for alcoholics grew into fellowships dealing with a host of behaviors and substance use.

It's also worth mentioning that there's a second book of great importance, titled *Twelve Steps and Twelve Traditions* (also known as the 12&12), which consists of essays that Bill worked out with a ghostwriter, a Jesuit scholar named Tom Powers, in the early 1950s. We'll talk more about the Traditions in a bit. The 12&12

is controversial in some AA circles—Joe and Charlie didn't like it because the newcomer *does* like it. Why does the newcomer like it? "Because the book doesn't make you do anything," they explained. The 12&12 talks about the Steps and Traditions and offers a lot of really great nuggets, but it also includes a lot of the sort of Freudian psychology for which Dr. Bob, and probably Bill as well, had no use for when the program began.

I'll tell you one quick story about the 12&12. One of the fellows at my home group, with whom I shared a sponsor, had been arrested for a domestic situation. Our joint sponsor, Milton, went to bail him out. As you can imagine, it can take hours for someone to be released from a correctional facility. The wait gave Milton the opportunity to read the 12&12 several times while waiting for my friend to emerge.

When he finally did, they started the long journey back to their homes. This story took place in Los Angeles. Anyone who knows the area will understand that traffic patterns being what they are, most trips involve being stuck in a traffic jam at some point. During the traffic-filled drive, Milton regaled my friend with tons of thoughts from the 12&12—a book Milton loves.

My friend, stuck listening to his sponsor talking endlessly about the 12&12, finally looked at him.

"Milton," he said plaintively, "take me back to jail." ■

Q. Why'd You Include All That Crazy Stuff about Bill and the Big Book?

A. Why have I shared bits and pieces of Bill's imperfections and the Big Book's imperfections as well? The worst thing that could happen to any Twelve Step program is if Bill and Dr. Bob are turned into something they weren't—perfect human beings. Or if the Big Book develops such iconic status that no one dares question or criticize a word. Bill was imperfect, and the Big Book is an imperfect guide to sobriety. But if you take the imperfect guidance this imperfect man put into this imperfect book, you will become perfectly sober. ▣

Q. Why Is There So Much Negative Stuff about Fellowships Online?

A. Hard to say. There are a lot of negative people in the world, some of whom are addicts and alcoholics, and some of them didn't like what they found "in the rooms." Maybe they went to a bad meeting or met a few blowhards who turned them off to recovery. Or maybe they didn't want to do the things required in a Twelve Step program (find a Higher Power, make amends, etc.). Or maybe . . . who knows.

It doesn't take much courage to write nasty things about Twelve Step recovery, or about anything else, online. Some people go to great trouble to construct elaborate websites dedicated to trashing fellowships. Sigh. Why put all that time into something so negative? Twelve Step recovery is pretty fabulous—it's the only thing that has worked for so many people over so much time. Is it perfect? Far from it. Sometimes I glance at those sites and I ask myself, what was so disappointing or upsetting for these individuals about NA, AA, MA, or some other A? What left them so bitter? I guess I'll never know, but I've got other fish to fry, like finishing this book for one thing. ■

What Are the Twelve Traditions, and Why Should I Care?

A. In the early, wild, and woolly days of Alcoholics Anonymous, there were no hard and fast rules for how individual meetings or the fellowship as a whole should operate. Nor was life in a Twelve Step program like it is today, where you can just find a meeting directory online and take a seat in the back. Initially, as we've talked about elsewhere, you had to take the first three Steps before they would even let you into a meeting. In some cities, you had to have a membership card. At times, there were dues, and you had to be a white, heterosexual male to join the program.

No, I'm not kidding.

Obviously things changed, but slowly and fitfully. To paraphrase the Big Book, remember that we're dealing with alcoholics, who are cunning, baffling, and powerful. With such potential for conflict, how would we all get along?

There's a famous story that makes the rounds in the fellowship that tells us how one group ended up posting sixty-one rules for its members, the complexity of which were ultimately swept away by rule sixty-two—don't take yourself too seriously. Sometimes today, Twelve Step members will say to each other, "Rule sixty-two," referencing that long-ago long list of dos and don'ts.

Eventually, people figured out what worked and didn't work, across the various fellowships. Part of that process started when Bill decided to codify the system by which the AA fellowship as a whole managed its affairs. He wanted to do this in time for AA's international convention in 1955, twenty years after its founding.

The question Bill faced: how do you get a bunch of unruly alcoholics to buy into a whole new set of rules?

Bill came up with a brilliant idea—or in his terminology, a *ten strike*—to call them *traditions* instead of calling them *rules*.

You have to laugh. Here's an organization that's only existed for twenty years, and suddenly it has a brand-new set of rules, but what are those rules called? Traditions. Typically, traditions are things that evolve over generations or even centuries. So here's Bill, pulling yet another fast one, getting the organization to buy into his thinking by tapping into the sense of history, loyalty, and virtue implied by the word *traditions*.

Do you really need to know about the Traditions right now? Not especially. Your sobriety will get along just fine without you having to study them. But if you're curious, it's said that the Traditions are to the fellowship as the Steps are to the group—the suggestions for having things go smoothly in life.

Perhaps the most important Tradition that applies to the newcomer is the Twelfth and last one—anonymity. When AA started—and remember that AA is the foundation for all the other Twelve Step programs—people would identify themselves on radio or in newspapers and magazines as members of Alcoholics Anonymous. Back then, the fellowship was so small that it only would take a sober celebrity or two to get drunk and damage the reputation of AA.

Then there's the question of how anonymity supports our humility in working our program. Bill himself faced a dilemma between his ego and his spirituality when *TIME* magazine invited him to have his face on the cover. Regretfully—deeply regretfully—he declined.*

And so the guideline remains to this day.

---

*By that same logic, I shouldn't have an author photo on this book. So I don't.

Anonymity protects the fellowship from the bad publicity that follows if someone slips or goes out, but it also protects the individual. It's really cool to be a sober member of the Twelve Step fellowship—but only within the rooms of the fellowship. In the outside world, not so much. Not everybody "gets it." Not everybody is thrilled for your sobriety. Anonymity means that you don't have to tell people that you're clean and sober in a Twelve Step program. It means that you get to live your sober life, and just as you do not disclose to others the names of the people you meet in meetings, those folks will also protect you. A lot of people are worried about the fact that "if I go to a meeting, people will see me." They forget that they're going to see a bunch of people managing the same disease. The only people who show up to meetings wearing sunglasses are movie stars who don't want to be noticed.

Of course they do.

So that's anonymity.

Another important Tradition is that groups are autonomous—they can govern themselves as they see fit, as long as they don't hurt the fellowship. There are groups that have a lot of weird rules. A few won't let you speak unless you have ten years of sobriety or more, or require that you take the Steps in the exact way that the other members in the group take the Steps, even if you are not wearing a suit and tie or a dress that covers your knees. It's fine. If you don't like those rules, go to a different meeting. Or start your own.

There's a joke in Twelve Step circles that all it takes to start a meeting is resentment and a coffee pot. It's hard to change the culture of a meeting that's been around for a while. If you're really uncomfortable, it's probably best to go elsewhere—or just see if you can live with however they do things in that group.

Another key Tradition keeps the fellowship "nonprofessional." The Eighth Tradition means that we don't get paid to do things in our Twelve Step groups; we're not compensated to speak, sponsor, set up chairs, or anything else. Central offices and inter-groups can hire typists, secretaries, webmasters, or whatever, but individual members do not receive financial compensation for what we do.

This is one of the best things about the program—it's not about the money. The groups are not trying to get your money, and there are actually limits to how much you can give. Everybody is asked to kick in a couple of bucks when the basket passes, and that money goes for rent, literature, and snacks. The fact that money is not a factor in the program and in the fellowship is a guarantee that the newcomer can trust it.

The funny thing about the Traditions is that they work really well. If you really want to get technical, there's something called the Twelve Concepts of Service, but you have to be a real Twelve Step nerd even to know they exist. Oops, I guess that includes me. Anyway, stick with the Steps for now, learn about the Traditions as you go along, and all will be well. ■

Q. Why Do People Relapse, and Will I?

A. Sober people get drunk or high (remember, don't call it relapse!) because the natural thing for addicts and alcoholics to do is drink and use. Sobriety is the unnatural act!

You hear a lot of reasons why people "go out," but for the most part, these are actually excuses. People drink and use again because it's what they're comfortable doing. It might be that it's how they saw their parents respond to stress, or because they were having a bad day because somebody looked at them funny and it really hurt. We're addicts. Addicts practice addictive behavior. That's the natural order of things. That's why I say that for an addict, sobriety is the unnatural act.

For us, there are neuropathways we have carved into our brains through addictive behaviors that we have repeated for years or decades. So "going out" is something against which every member of a Twelve Step program must be on guard.

In a South Boston meeting years ago, I heard a member caution the group to "Respect the opponent." When I heard this for the first time, it resonated with me. Personally, I take that to mean that I can't take the disease lightly.

As I write these words, I'm thinking about a funeral I attended recently; it was the funeral of a twenty-three-year-old who overdosed on opioids (as if there were a proper dose that he should have administered to himself).

He was born about a year and a half after I got sober. And now he is gone.

Could he have lived?

I cannot answer in his specific case, but I can certainly offer some thoughts about you and me. If we are diligent about the Steps, if we are sponsored and carry the message to others, if we make our amends, if we attend meetings regularly, if we have a home group, if we pray and meditate, if we read the literature of our specific Twelve Step program or programs, and if we generally try to act like decent people to ourselves and to others, we stand a much better chance of staying sober.

The Big Book promises that we are placed in a "position of neutrality" with regard to alcohol if we are alcoholics, and other Twelve Step programs essentially offer the same thing. But we only stay neutral toward alcohol or other substances or behaviors as long as we remain in what the Big Book calls "fit spiritual condition."

In that sense, going out is a choice, and it's a choice we typically make days or even months before we actually pick up the drink, the drug, the cigarette, the bowl of ice cream, the new lover, whatever our "drug of choice" might be.

We make the decision to get drunk or high, and then we wait for the opportunity when we can act on that decision.

In fact, my sponsor says that from the time we make a decision to go out, we actually stop taking the Steps in descending order.

We stop carrying the message—that's when we quit taking the Twelfth Step. Then we stop praying and meditating, so we're no longer doing Step Eleven.

Then we stop being accountable for our actions, so we're no longer taking Step Ten.

And so on, until we have let go of our relationship to our Higher Power and are essentially sponsoring ourselves.

This is a recipe for disaster.

In fact, we are not "stuck" high or drunk. If you do what you're supposed to do, you will be placed, so the Big Book tells us, in a "position of neutrality" with regard to alcohol (and other drugs). You may have the occasional desire, but the compulsion to drink or use will have been removed. So if you're fortunate enough to find your way into a Twelve Step program, stay there. Work your program. Live the Steps. And your chances of going back out will be very low. ■

A. "One day at a time" has always been one of the most important mantras in Alcoholics Anonymous, and as Twelve Step programs have grown, it's become a popular phrase across the board. It makes sense when you think about it. Ever heard the expression "Life's hard by the yard but it's a cinch by the inch"? It's true. Life is a series of days, and we can only live in this one day. So if we focus our efforts on staying sober today, and then wash, rinse, and repeat tomorrow, we can stay clean and sober.

The idea of never drinking again and never using again is just too big and overwhelming. It's possible that Bill Wilson, when he came up with the "One day at a time" concept, was reading Dale Carnegie, author of the perennially popular book *How to Win Friends and Influence People*. Carnegie, one of the most famous self-help authors of all time, advised, "Live your life in day-tight compartments." In other words, don't try to solve all the problems of your life, or make all the money you'll ever need, or figure out your relationship, or straighten things out with your parents, or buy a new house, all in one day. Just do what you can today, and let the future take care of itself.

It does make sense. Alcoholics and addicts tend to live in the past, resentfully reminding ourselves of all the wrongs that others have done us. Or we live in the future, projecting the dire consequences likely to follow from the miserable position in which we find ourselves today.

There's one place where addicts are highly uncomfortable, and that's the present moment. That's why we do everything we can to escape the present, by drinking and drugging, by betting and spending, through food and sex. It's also why page 59 of the Big Book says, "May you find Him [your Higher Power] now!"

Now. In the moment. Today.

Today is the only day in which we live. Doesn't that sound obvious? And yet, we do absolutely everything we can to get out of the moment and relive an unhappy past or project an equally unhappy future. What if we were to take seriously the concept of living one day at a time, truly buying into the idea that our life would be better if we just focused on the moment in which we find ourselves?

I know. You're thinking, "How Zen of you, Michael."

In fact, since today is all we have, and tomorrow is not promised, what if we were to just simply stay sober today instead of worrying about the rest of our lives? "One day at a time" has been a successful strategy in AA for more than eighty years. That's why the idea has been integrated into Twelve Step practice by all the organizations ending in A.

So yes, when we talk about "a day at a time"—we really mean it. A life in recovery is lived a day at a time. Period. If you can stay sober the rest of your life without staying sober today, then I should be reading your book! ■

A. Here's another wonderful old AA slogan for you: "It's the engine that gets you, not the caboose." Meaning it's the first drink, drug, or substitute that gets you in trouble, not the seventh, eighth, or ninth.

This simple idea is actually revolutionary from the perspective of most alcoholics and addicts. We tell ourselves that "this time, I'll only . . ." I'll only have one or two drinks. It will only be a few hits. A couple bumps. Whatever your poison, "this time" will be different. But before long, we've gone way past that "just one or two." Reflecting the classic formulation presented in the Big Book, before long we're "beating on the bar," wondering how on earth we overshot the mark and either used or drank five or ten times more than we had intended.

"The Doctor's Opinion" at the beginning of the Big Book provides a phrase that pretty much every sober alcoholic and addict can buy in to: "the phenomenon of craving." The first drink, the first use, the first step into old behaviors sets off a calling in the body for the next and the next and the next. We drink or use until we've run out of alcohol or other drugs. That escalates until we pass out, are restrained, are arrested, or in some cases, die. The whole emphasis is on believing and practicing that we cannot drink or use moderately on a consistent basis. So the focus of the program is avoiding the first drink, the very first use.

If you combine the idea of "One day at a time" with the idea that it's the "engine and not the caboose"—that it's the first drink or use that gets you into trouble, because that's what sets off the phenomenon of craving—you end up with the idea that AA was set up to answer the following calls for help: "Please keep me from one drink for one day." That translates to "Please keep me from using for one day." "Please keep me from overeating for one day." "Please keep me from gambling for one day."

You get the idea. Again, pick your poison. Apply it to the idea.

You can boil down all of Twelve Step practice to that simple phrase. Only it's not so simple. Please keep me from one drink, one use—which one? The first drink. The first use. Why? Because the very first one sets off the phenomenon of craving. Why do we say it's a phenomenon? Because it's unusual. "Normal" drinkers and normal users don't have this phenomenon. Only we lucky few. For one day. Why one? Because we live one day at a time, we get and stay clean and sober one day at a time, or we're back to suicide on the installment plan, which means drinking and using and therefore dying one day at a time.

At heart, the program is simple. The principles of the program work for anyone. That's the beauty of Twelve Step programs.

When I first got sober, I remember looking around the room and thinking, "I know this works for all of you people, but how do I know it's going to work for me?"

I also thought about the old joke about the guy who was strapped to the electric chair, and he looks up at his executioner and he says, "Are you sure this thing is safe?"

It's safe.

And real life is a lot safer when you are asking to be kept from the first drink, the first use, for nothing more than one day. ◾

Q. Why Do I Have to Have a Higher Power?

A. Among the fellowship, it is said that the song "My Way" is the loser's national anthem.

Alcoholism and addiction are lonely diseases. We say that our disease wants to get us alone so it can kill us. Most addicts and alcoholics, even those who enjoy the bar scene, are natural-born loners, leery of human companionship unless the people with whom they are interacting are capable of providing alcohol and other drugs, shelter, money, or sex.

It's often pointed out in Twelve Step meetings that the first word of the Twelve Steps is we, as in, "it's a we program." Alone we drink or use and die; together we get and stay clean and sober. Relying on our own limited selves for sobriety has proven to be ineffective. As Albert Einstein said, "The same mind that created the problem cannot solve the problem."*

Whether Einstein said it or not, it makes sense. If I have an alcoholic or addictive mind, and my mind is the sole basis for deciding whether or not I'm going to stay sober today, there's an awfully good chance that I won't. I'll use because, well, that's what I like to do. It's comfortable, it's familiar, it kills pain—it's a very successful strategy.

Of course, that success comes with a price—nearly everything worth living for. Love. Self-respect. Education. Community.

---

*The beauty of attributing a statement to Einstein is that it becomes irrefutable. Who the hell are you to argue with Albert Einstein?

Family. You name it, crumble it up, and mix it into your poison of choice, because you'll be drinking (or smoking or snorting) whatever you love along with your favorite substance.

So if our own minds cannot keep us clean and sober, what can?

The answer in Twelve Step land: a Higher Power greater than ourselves.

The Big Book is explicit. It essentially declares the purpose of the book is to help you find a Power greater than yourself that will keep you sober. In other words, the fundamental idea of Twelve Step recovery is that I cannot keep myself clean and sober, but something else can.

Something bigger and stronger than my disease. Something bigger and stronger than I.

And this is where a lot of newcomers struggle and often give up.

The whole Higher Power thing is so dispiriting. The book even acknowledges this fact. On page 45 of the Big Book, it says, "Many times we talk to a new man and watch his hope rise as we discuss his alcoholic problems and explain our fellowship. But his face falls when we speak of spiritual matters, especially when we mention God, for we have re-opened a subject which our man thought he had neatly evaded or entirely ignored."

In other words, AA is a program rooted in spirituality—and so is every program modeled after it.

Not religion per se. You can have a religion or no religion and do perfectly well in Alcoholics Anonymous. Instead, we are talking about your own spirit. As we discussed earlier, the great psychologist Carl Jung called alcohol "a low-level quest for God." That's why another word for alcohol is . . . *spirits!* Many religions around the world use alcohol or other drugs as a means of achieving ecstasy or raising one's spirit. Twelve Step programs use *spirit* as a way of arresting the need to drink or use.

How does it work? No one's really sure. If you ask an old-timer how it works, he'll respond with a derisive snort. "It works fine."*

It's a very hard thing for many alcoholics or addicts to believe, but the same Power that created you, whether you want to call it God or the universe or something else—that same Power loves you, wants you to succeed, and will help you with your addiction problem, if only you will let it. Chuck C., an early member of AA in southern California and another of my grand-sponsors, used to say, "God is a gentleman. He doesn't go where he isn't invited."

So it's up to us to let our Higher Power in.

I know it's hard. It was hard for me, and it's hard for most of us. Even people who already believe in the existence of God have a hard time believing that their Higher Power cares enough about them to help them stay sober. After all, if there is a God, why did he let us slip so far down? Why didn't he protect us?

The simple fact is that God gave people free will, and if you're going to exercise your free will in a way that's self-destructive, don't look for God to throw a rope around your waist and keep you from running off to the dealer man. And if you want to blame God for all the tragedy that exists in the world, feel free. But ultimately, like it or not, your Higher Power is the only game in town if you want to get clean and stay clean.

Think of it this way. Here you are. If you look down, you'll see alcohol and other drugs, a lower form of a Higher Power. Something that isn't exactly beneficial to you at this point in the game. Now look up. There's your higher Higher Power. Again, whether you use the term *God, Higher Power, spirit of the universe,* or whatever, it's a higher Higher Power than the lower Higher Power of drugs and alcohol, wouldn't you agree?

So through our program, we are not choosing between

---

*How I hated those old-timers with their derisive snorts. Now that I'm one, I try very hard not to snort derisively within twenty-five feet of any newcomer.

surrendering and not surrendering. We are choosing between surrendering to a lower Higher Power of drugs and alcohol or a higher Higher Power of spirituality, however we define *spirituality*.

And that's one of the most exciting things—and biggest challenges—within a Twelve Step program. No one is going to tell you what your Higher Power must be. Instead, you've got to figure that out for yourself. Other people will be happy to talk with you about it, but at the end of the day, it's your call. The Big Book language uses traditional, masculine terms for God, but you don't have to. As we have seen, you can call your Higher Power whatever you want.

Let's examine in greater depth the story of Ebby Thatcher, a childhood friend of AA cofounder Bill Wilson, who visited Bill in his Brooklyn apartment in late 1934. Bill had tried and failed repeatedly to stay sober, and he was sitting in his apartment drinking gin, essentially waiting to die.

Bill was delighted that Ebby had come to visit because they could drink together. Instead, Ebby shared remarkable news— he had found religion and, therefore, no longer found it necessary to drink. Bill was initially disappointed that his old drinking buddy had switched from being an alcoholic crackpot to a religious crackpot, but Bill was delighted nonetheless to sit and talk with him, figuring that his gin would last longer than his friend's religious rantings.

To Bill's surprise, what Ebby said made sense to him. Ebby had found a spiritual solution for his alcoholism in the Oxford Group—an early twentieth-century movement that took a special interest in the problem of alcoholism. Ebby told Bill, in effect, that if he would ask for spiritual help, he wouldn't have to drink again. That was the solution Ebby had found. Somehow, the idea made sense in Bill's gin-addled brain. The thing that really blew away Bill was the idea Ebby shared that "you can choose your own conception of God."

In other words, recovery is not based on acceptance of anyone else's religious beliefs. You don't have to believe the dogma you heard growing up in your church, synagogue, or mosque. You don't have to "buy" anyone else's ideas about God. As we've said, all you have to know about a Higher Power, as Ebby suggested, is that you have one, and that you're not it.

Bill talked about how the concept of choosing one's own Higher Power electrified him. He ended up drinking one more time and found himself back in Towns Hospital, a drying-out spot for drunks that was in Manhattan. But by that time, the idea of defining one's Higher Power in personal terms had given Bill a new approach to spirituality. This one conversation with Ebby put him on a path toward cofounding Alcoholics Anonymous.

What made the difference? The idea that Bill could choose his own Higher Power. And so did I, and so did you.

Look, they call it a *leap* of faith, not a *crawl* of faith. If you don't believe that something bigger than yourself can keep you sober, then try to find belief in the fact that I believe, and that millions of sober alcoholics and addicts around the world also believe. If you want to make a start in Twelve Step recovery, do what Ebby asked Bill to do—lay aside any prejudices you have about what God may be and instead ask that being to support you as you begin your own quest for sobriety.

As the cheerfully antisocial old-timers will tell you, "If it doesn't work, we will cheerfully refund your misery within thirty days."

They call that "the AA guarantee."

But I'll give you another one that's even better. If you do the simple things the program asks you to do, a day at a time, you'll never have to drink or use again, if you don't want to, and as my friend Jerry D. says, you'll never have to be lonely again, if you don't want to.

And that's a guarantee you can take to the bank. ▪

You Don't Get It, Michael. I Really Don't Like God. Now What?

A. I hear you.

Let me tell you my own story. About a month after my tenth birthday, my parents called us into the big bedroom. You know what I mean: When you are a kid, and you get called into the sanctity of your parents' bedroom, you somehow know the talk you are about to hear will change your life. My mother said, "Grandpa is very sick. We may not see him again."

What she didn't tell my sisters and me was that my grandpa had been murdered in a mob hit the night before, strangled to death in his hotel room in Chicago, because he was a diamond dealer who had been fingered to the mob as someone who carried a large amount of stones when he traveled.

My grandmother learned the news not from a compassionate social worker or police officer but instead from a *New York Post* reporter, who called her in the middle of the night to ask her for her reaction to the murder, of which, until that moment, she knew nothing.

Keep in mind that my mother's parents had escaped the Nazi Holocaust by the skin of their teeth and that all of their relatives, with the exception of my grandfather's brother and sister, young and old, were murdered by the Nazis in the extermination camps.

And then this is how my grandfather dies.

For my grandmother, who lost her parents and five siblings to the Nazis, this was the final straw. Shortly after, she developed breast cancer and died after a four-year struggle with the disease, during which time my mother had to be by her side more and more, not just to take her to doctors and hospitals but also to run the diamond importing business that my grandfather had started and that my grandmother had taken over. Through all of this, my father essentially lost my mother to her caregiving responsibilities; he began to drink and see other women. My sisters and I developed into full-blown alcoholics and addicts by the time we were out of high school. And you're going to tell me that *you* don't like God? We've all got our reasons for coming to terms with a Higher Power; I'm sure you've got yours as well.

Years later, I find myself in Twelve Step recovery, where I'm told, as you are now, that my recovery depends on my willingness and ability to do business with a Higher Power.

I want to share with you how I was able to overcome my antipathy toward God, and how I was able to start to do business with a Higher Power, so that I wouldn't die of this disease. Like you, I didn't see how that was possible. So I want to share with you what I learned along the way, which ultimately made a big difference for me. Not just a big difference—all the difference.

I realized that I had two major problems with the idea of God—the first was that I was angry at God for the things that had happened in my family and in everybody else's family, and the second is that I was ashamed of the things that I had done. After all, if there is a God, God had seen them, and I didn't think I could really show my face to a Higher Power after the things I had done.

After a while, I realized that if there were a God, He had given people free will. Free will means you can do the right thing or the wrong thing. And then one day the realization hit—just as I could not blame God for the wrong things I had done to other people, I realized I could no longer blame God for the things that had happened to my family or to anyone else.

What about kids who develop cancer, or the Holocaust, or terror attacks? What do I tell myself about all that?

I came to realize that those things are tragedy, and tragedy has no explanation. It can be a teacher, but I'm not smart enough to explain why tragedy exists. All I know is that the existence of tragedy does not preclude the existence of God.

In other words, a loving God can preside over a world that includes tragedy. I don't have the intellectual capacity to explain how that could be, or why that could be, but I do have enough of a brain to tell you that one thing does not rule out the other.

As the expression goes, the believer only has to have faith in the existence of God. The atheist has to explain everything else.

All I have to explain, therefore, and somehow come to terms with, is the coexistence of God and tragedy. The nonbeliever has to explain absolutely everything else in existence, from the one-celled amoeba to the mind of man.

Go ahead. I'll wait.

That's how I was able to come to terms with the anger I had toward God. Now what about the shame I felt?

One of the first things I heard in AA was that "I wasn't that good at being that bad." In other words, all of the things that I had done that were wrong were pretty much the sort of wrong things that lots of other people have done. I'm not justifying my actions—I'm just saying that I didn't do anything that rose to a new level of horror or crime. I had to get over the shame I felt toward God, if I were going to do business with Him, and the starting point for me was first forgiving myself, recognizing that "I wasn't that good at being that bad." Nothing I did was so terrible that it could not be forgiven.

There's this phrase that used to be pretty commonly used in the rooms of recovery—"the Lindbergh baby syndrome." If you were suffering from this syndrome, it meant you felt guilty not only for the things that you've done but also for pretty much any-thing else bad that ever happened in the world, up to and including the kidnapping of aviator Charles Lindbergh's baby, which was considered one of the major crimes of the twentieth century. Alcoholics and addicts sometimes feel guilty just for breathing, that we don't even deserve air.

When you think about the background I came from and all the things that my family endured, it's a wonder that I didn't come out any worse. But whatever I had done, I had to forgive myself, and I had to seek forgiveness from others in the Eighth and Ninth Steps. And I did that. I made amends to at least sixty people—employers, ex-girlfriends, family members, roommates, friends, a hotel staff, and a movie theater staff. I had quite the temper back then. (Still do, alas. It just doesn't flare up quite as often, or quite as virulently.)

I could not un-ring the bell, make the things I'd done of which I was ashamed disappear. But I could go back to the people I had harmed and apologize, and I could also commit to myself not to behave in the same manner if a similar situation arose again.

And that's what I did, and that's how I was able to eliminate the shame I felt about the things that I had done.

So there you have it. The anger I felt at God I was able to resolve in this manner: God created the world. God created people and gave them free will. Just as I used my free will to harm others, and I cannot blame God for what I did, so I cannot blame God for the ways in which other people used their free will to harm me or the people I loved.

This was very freeing for me. It might help you, or perhaps it might inspire you to look at whatever stands in the way of your relationship with a Higher Power.

The shame side was simpler—it all came down to forgiveness. Forgiving myself, and seeking forgiveness from others. The ability to put my head on the pillow at night with a relatively clean conscience was as wonderful a sensation as not waking up in the morning hungover. I wish the same for you.

Again, you may have your own reasons for hating God. They may make mine look like child's play by comparison. The point is this: Whatever stands in the way of your relationship with your Higher Power, it's time to examine it and decide whether whatever hatred or fear or resentment of God is worth hanging on to, at the likely cost of your sobriety. Of your life. I'm not here to make that decision for you. I certainly made mine, and I don't regret it.

Do I still harbor resentment toward God and toward the persons who killed my grandfather? Or to the perpetrators of the Holocaust? Or to terrorists? Of course. These are things I think about frequently. But I don't dwell on them, and I don't let my negativity about those things dominate my life. I'm able to be a loving husband and father, a servant-leader in my business, a member of my Twelve Step community, a member of my religious community, and a citizen who pays his taxes and shows up for life.

You can think of early sobriety as a series of gut checks for the newly clean individual. Am I willing to go to a meeting? That's a gut check. Am I willing to stop drinking and using? That's a gut check. Am I willing to contemplate the idea of a Higher Power in my life? That's a gut check.

The suggestion I offer: don't stop now. Whether you continue or resume the faith of your upbringing is your business. Whether you stay sober is the business of you and your Higher Power, so whatever stands in the way of that relationship, I hope you'll take time to think it through. ■

Q. Who Were the "Three Doctors" Who Influenced the Program?

A. If you've never listened to "The Big Book Comes Alive," the Joe and Charlie program on the Big Book of Alcoholics Anonymous, you're missing something great. When I got sober, I had to order the cassettes, and then put them on my Walkman.* That was a long time ago. Today, you can find their show online for free in a variety of places. So give up Facebook for a few hours and tune in to Joe and Charlie.

If I could change one thing about Twelve Step recovery,† I would ban smartphones from the rooms. Not just their use during the meeting—and I confess that sometimes when I'm really bored or antsy, I will check out something on my own phone—but before and after the meeting as well. It used to be that you came into a meeting room and everybody was talking.

There were little conversation clumps here and there. Big meetings offered the same friendly, expectant buzz you heard when you entered a good bar.

Today, by contrast, because of smartphones, stepping into a Twelve Step meeting room is like stepping into the public library. Nobody's talking. Everybody's just sitting there, atomized, spacing out on their smartphones, getting the dopamine high that an ongoing flow of fresh information provides.

---

*As the expression goes, I'm dating myself, but I'm not sleeping with myself.

†There I go again.

It's antisocial. It's no fun. There's no exchange of ideas, no flirting, none of the socializing that the fellowship traditionally offered. Alcoholics and addicts need to know how to hold conversations with other people. We know how to get over on people. We know how to connive. We know how to beg for sex without making it look like we're begging for sex. But the art of conversation is rapidly becoming a lost art for folks like us, because people sit down, take out their phones, and punch away. If I didn't know better, I'd swear people were staring at their own genitals, because most people tend to keep the phone right over their private parts, like the fig leaf in a medieval painting. If I could change one thing about Twelve Step recovery, it would be to ban phones from meeting rooms.

It's not just banter and the development of essential social skills that's lost. It's much harder to identify a newcomer. When you've got five members talking over here, and three members talking over there, and one guy standing there with a cup of coffee and a deeply uncomfortable look, it's easy to spot the newcomer, whether it's your home group or not. There he is—the guy I need to go over and talk to.

What do you say to a potential newcomer? Ask him how his day is going. Ask if this is his home group. Ask if he's been in the program a long time. Get his phone number. Give him yours. The presence of smartphones in the halls diminishes the ability of members to carry on Twelve Step work, because newcomers are just as buried in their smartphones as are the old-timers.

But I digress.

I mentioned Joe and Charlie here because they made a fascinating point about the early history of AA: that the fellowship owes a great debt to three physicians, who were neither alcoholics nor addicts themselves. Let's take a look at who these fine gentlemen were, what they offered the nascent AA fellowship and Twelve Step recovery in general, and why they still matter today.

Contrary to myth, the program did not emerge suddenly and completely from the forehead of its wise cofounder, Bill W. Bill's genius, and it was genius, consisted in stitching together vital ideas from a variety of sources that, taken together, became the foundational ideas of AA. Joe and Charlie pointed out that three MDs, all nonalcoholics, were the sources of some of these key ideas. Let's look at each in turn.

We've talked a lot about the concept of the spiritual awakening and how essential it is to real recovery in Twelve Step programs. But where did the concept come from? The answer is Carl Jung, the pioneering Swiss psychologist who recognized that there was more to people's inner lives than the Freudian complexes that dominated the conversation about human psychology during the early twentieth century.

Jung grasped that people were more than bundles of subconscious, suppressed sexual desires and other seemingly negative traits. Jung was a psychologist who recognized that human beings had souls.

So what's the connection between AA and Dr. Jung?

In the late 1920s, a wealthy American businessman, Rowland Hazard III, or Rowland H. to folks like us, uprooted his entire family from New York to Switzerland so that he could have Dr. Jung treat his alcoholism, for which, up until then, he had found no cure. After a year of work with Rowland, Dr. Jung broke the sad news, the story of which is recounted in chapter 2 of the Big Book.

Jung told Rowland there was nothing medical science could do to cure his alcoholism. The only solution Jung knew of was to employ "huge emotional displacements and rearrangements" of a spiritual nature. That, Jung said, was the only hope that Rowland or any alcoholic or addict had for recovering from the "seemingly hopeless state of mind and body" known as active alcoholism.

Rowland returned to the United States and found his way into the Oxford Group, seeking a spiritual solution. The Oxford Group, which we've talked about earlier, formed "drunk squads," whose mission it was to convince alcoholics to stop drinking. Rowland, freshly returned from his stand with Dr. Jung, entered the Oxford Group and had the kind of spiritual awakening that would later be described in the Twelfth Step.

He then turned around and helped get sober none other than Ebby Thatcher, who visited Bill's apartment a few months later and carried the good news that he had gotten sober, and so could Bill.

So that's the chain of events—Dr. Jung to Rowland to Ebby to Bill and, decades later, from their successors to you and me. We are the beneficiaries of that early connection between Jung and what would become Alcoholics Anonymous, which was used as the foundation for hundreds of other Twelve Step programs.

Bill Wilson actually entered into correspondence with Dr. Jung. There is a degree of controversy surrounding the correspondence they allegedly shared. There's a letter in Bill's archives purportedly from Dr. Jung, expounding on a concept of a spiritual awakening as it pertains to alcoholics. People who really study these matters will tell you that the rubber stamp used to sign that letter was not something Jung used in the decade that he wrote that letter, calling into question its legitimacy.

The bottom line, however, is that Jung's influence on the program remains intact to this day: the need for a spiritual reorganizing, or awakening, in order to counter alcoholism and addiction. Imagine how dismal Twelve Step recovery would have been had Sigmund Freud, and not Carl Jung, been its primary source of psychological and spiritual belief.

Since Freud believed in analysis, our Fourth Step would have been the First Step, which means that alcoholics and addicts would have been launched into self-examination even before they had understood or accepted the need for spiritual help. So let me go on record as saying that I'm grateful that Freud did not have a hand in early AA.

In Dr. Bob's final speech, he addressed the issue squarely: "Let's not mess this up with Freudian complexes," he told his audience, words that hang in a thousand Twelve Step meeting rooms.

As a result, Twelve Step recovery, no matter how old it gets, remains forever Jung.*

The second nonalcoholic MD to whom the program owes an enormous debt is the founder of the Oxford Group, Dr. Frank Buchman. The idea behind the Oxford Group was that people needed to dedicate themselves to honest, sincere, spiritually pure living. If people were better, Buchman reasoned, the world would be better. He created for his members a six-step program toward that better way of life.

As we have seen, Bill took Buchman's six steps, applied them directly to the problem of alcoholism, and doubled their number to twelve. If it had not been for the second nonalcoholic doctor, Frank Buchman, Alcoholics Anonymous would never have had a concept of Steps upon which to draw.

Amusingly, I once heard an audio recording that stated that Bill deliberately chose the word *took* as in, "these are the steps we took," reasoning that alcoholics are *takers*. Told they would have to *work* the Twelve Steps, they would have been too lazy, but taking is right in their wheelhouse.

The third of the nonalcoholic doctors who provided pivotal guidance to AA was Dr. William Silkworth, who ran the drying-out hospital for drunks where Bill would repair when he had gone on a particularly bad bender. Think of it as Airbnb for people with good credit and bad hangovers. Silkworth and Bill apparently became very good friends—Bill was there often enough.

One of the most important moments in AA history came after Bill had experienced his life-changing visit with Ebby. In fact, it wasn't life changing enough for Bill to quit drinking on the spot.

---

*Couldn't resist.

He went on one more spree, to use the then-popular term, and landed in a bed once again in Dr. Silkworth's Towns Hospital. There, defeated by alcoholism for the umpteenth time and convinced that he was going to finally die of the disease, he thought back on his conversation with Ebby and commanded that God reveal himself.

Bill then had a sudden spiritual transformation—a literal white light experience that shifted his entire being. God came to him suddenly, as he later recounted, both in the Big Book and countless times in front of AA audiences. (You can find Bill's story, which he named "The Bedtime Story," online; he took two hours to tell his story, punctuated by a ten-minute cigarette break.)

Dr. Silkworth also realized that Bill was a changed man. Bill, a hopeless alcoholic to that point, never drank again. He died in 1971.*

Dr. Silkworth and Bill both recognized that Bill's "white light experience" was transformative. Bill left Towns Hospital shortly thereafter with his sobriety and a new plan. He then threw himself into the idea of convincing other alcoholics to quit drinking by pursuing the same sort of spiritual experience that Bill had enjoyed. If you can imagine this, Bill barhopping, trying to persuade drunks on barstools to give up their alcohol and follow his path. Unsurprisingly, Bill converted exactly no one to sobriety.

He went back to Towns Hospital—not as a patient but rather to detail to Dr. Silkworth his feelings of failure in helping others to stay sober. Dr. Silkworth pointed out the obvious—by trying to carry a message to other drunks, Bill had stayed sober himself. And this was the third leg of the stool, a barstool, if you like, of AA principles—the idea that when you carry the message to others, you are enhancing your own recovery.

---

*He did become interested in LSD, the taking of which, in the 1960s, was not considered a slip.

Dr. Silkworth conveyed the idea to Bill that alcoholism was a disease, not a moral issue. This was a huge shift, because until then, if you were an alcoholic or an addict, you were a bad, weak, even evil person. No longer. Dr. Silkworth singlehandedly removed the moral stigma from addiction, an idea Bill popularized through Alcoholics Anonymous.

This is the third of the ideas from the three nonalcoholic doctors that Bill synthesized and from which he created Alcoholics Anonymous.

To recap: You've got the idea of the spiritual awakening, from Dr. Jung. You've got the concept of a Step-based recovery program, from Dr. Buchman and the Oxford Group. And you've got the idea of alcoholism and addiction as a disease and not a moral issue, impressed upon Bill by Dr. Silkworth at Towns Hospital.

Bill didn't invent AA from whole cloth. His genius—and I use that word again, and purposefully—consisted in recognizing the value of those three ideas and how, when combined, they created the atmosphere in which AA grew and prospered.

Bill was a lot of things—not all of them pleasant. In short, he was a complicated man. He was human. But could any other human being have recognized and combined those three vital ideas into a fairly simple approach to recovering from one of the worst problems that human beings face?

God bless Bill W. He recognized essential concepts when he saw them, and he put them together the way probably no one else could have. That's why we love him. Yes, that's why we still love Bill.

Okay, so now you know a ton about Twelve Step programs. But the Big Book chapter isn't called "Into Knowing" or "Into Thinking." It's called "Into Action." So let's get into action . . . and actually take those first three Steps. ▪

PART 2

Stepping It Up

Taking Steps One, Two, and Three

Now that you see how the Twelve Steps
might help you get and stay sober, one day
at a time, it's time to dig into the first three
Steps. As we've discussed, they're the
foundation for recovery. So let's take some
steps toward . . . taking the Steps.

What Does the Word *Powerless* in Step One Mean?

A. "We admitted we were powerless over alcohol—that our lives had become unmanageable." Alcoholics and addicts often struggle with the idea that they might be alcoholics and addicts. How ironic: Only alcoholics and addicts would wonder if they really were alcoholics or addicts. Nonalcoholics and nonaddicts never wonder about this. The mere fact that you are asking the question about yourself points to the answer.

So what does *powerless over alcohol* (or powerless over your drug of choice, be it marijuana, cocaine, heroin, debting, spending, sex, or people) really mean?

The simplest answer is that you cannot use your drug of choice "in safety."

And yet, the newcomer often says, "But I don't get in trouble every time I use. Sometimes it's okay."

And sometimes it isn't. The problem is that when things go badly, they can go really badly.

This morning, I was chatting with my Uber driver on my way to the airport. She said that an hour ago, she had picked up a woman in a decent part of town—this is around three in the morning, mind you. The woman said that she had been on a date, and they had been drinking, and the date disappeared, so she went to sleep on a bench.

That's not a good date.

Does that young lady go to sleep on a bench every time she drinks? Probably not.

But it only takes one time for disaster to happen.

Friends in my home group knew a guy who got drunk one night, got behind the wheel of a car, and killed a man in a head-on collision. The entire incident took place during an alcoholic blackout. When he regained consciousness, he was in a jail cell, with no recollection of the fatal accident.

He was sentenced to twenty-three years in prison.

A friend of mine in the program, an individual who adopted our family dog when my kids lost interest in it, had a consistently entertaining approach to AA, and I always enjoyed listening to him share. One day, he started interrupting other people while they were speaking, a big *faux pas* in Twelve Step land. His behavior became increasingly erratic. People in the group thought he had been drinking again and perhaps going off whatever medications he might have been taking to stabilize his mood. We can't be certain that he was drinking and using again, but it sure seemed that way.

One day, a woman in her seventies was walking her dog on the sidewalk in front of his home.

Enraged for whatever reason, he flew out of his house, stark naked, and beat the woman so severely that she was hospitalized and near death.

He's looking at thirteen years behind bars. Again, for an event he can't even recall.

Powerless doesn't mean that every time you drink or use, catastrophe ensues. It does mean, however, that the *possibility* for catastrophe ensues. In other words, any day could be your unlucky day.

People say you cannot scare an alcoholic or addict, so I'm not going to try. I've been "yeah, but"-ed enough to recognize the futility of the endeavor. The newcomer says, if not out loud, at least to himself or herself, "I've driven drunk or high hundreds of times. Nothing ever happened. I'll be fine."

That's the voice of your disease. Plain and simple.

Let me repeat that, just so it sinks in, in **bold-faced** type, because we addicts and alcoholics can take a while to catch on to something new. **That voice you've heard that has given you permission for everything has been your disease talking. Are you going to keep listening and giving up your power, your life, to your substance of choice—to your disease?**

Powerless doesn't mean that you will get into trouble every time, or even at any time. It does mean that you cannot control the outcome of events once you start drinking. Earlier we discussed the concept that "The first drink gets you drunk," because that first drink or pill or snort or bump sets off what Dr. Silkworth called in "The Doctor's Opinion" in the Big Book, "the phenomenon of craving." Your boring, nonalcoholic friend has half a drink and says, "I'm starting to feel it" and stops drinking.

Your reaction: Do you think anyone would notice if you finished his drink? Alcohol is not intrinsically bad. There's nothing wrong with a nice glass of wine or a tumbler of unblended scotch, if you can handle it—if you're not an alcoholic. I don't know too many people who can really be counted as social cocaine or heroin users, but there are a lot of people out there who can drink in safety. I'm just not one of them, and if you've read this far, chances are, neither are you. Champagne on New Year's Eve, a wedding toast, a carafe of wine at dinner—most enjoyable, if you're not one of us. If you are, there is nothing to stop you from drinking so much that bad consequences of some sort can happen.

What about nonalcoholic beer, you may ask. Well, we say that nonalcoholic beer is for nonalcoholics. In other words, don't dance with your disease.

Many people report that when they drink or use, they feel taller, more attractive, and sexier. Their inhibitions loosen, and they are able to march right up to that attractive person across the proverbial crowded room and flirt away.

My problem was that when I drank, I thought I was funny. I wasn't. I was just cutting and cruel.

Even if I didn't get behind the wheel of a car and put myself and others at risk, I was just a jerk.

There's one amend I can never make, and I still wince at the memory of it. I was having dinner with my then-girlfriend's family. It really looked as though this was *The One* and we were going to get married. Making a good impression was a good idea.

I didn't.

My future mother-in-law showed me a photo of my girlfriend when she was about six or seven years old.

"She was a cute child, wasn't she?" Mom asked.

I shook my head. "She was really ugly," I said, waiting for a laugh from the rest of the table—her immediate family—that never came.

Why can't I make that amend?

Because by the time I got sober, she had most likely gotten married to someone else, and she did not need her life disrupted by hearing from me again. (If you disagree, call my sponsor.)

After all, the Step says that we do not make amends when the amend itself will cause further harm.

Instead, I've had to live with that.

It may not sound like much, but I can still see, in my mind's eye, plain as day, the look of absolute shock, hurt, and disillusionment in the eyes of my potential mother-in-law and fiancée.

So the harm we cause when we drink or use doesn't have to be criminal in nature. We just hurt people.

We can hurt them badly.

I don't want to do that anymore. And probably neither do you.

Sometimes newcomers wonder if they drank or used enough, or often enough, to qualify for a given Twelve Step program.

I had a housemate years ago who was sober in AA. She used to say that it only took a sip of alcohol or a single puff on a joint for her to get high. But she knew she was an alcoholic and an addict, and she maintained solid sobriety in AA.

It's not how often you drank, either. Some people think they could not be alcoholic because they only drink on weekends, or on Mother's Day, or on days ending in Y.

Such alcoholics and addicts could be termed *periodic*. It means that they only drink or use on a sporadic basis, but a periodic alcoholic is an alcoholic nonetheless.

One of my best friends bought a home safe that operated with a time-lock feature. He kept his marijuana in the safe and would set the door to open every Friday at 4:00 p.m. The rest of the week, he couldn't get high, because he had no access. Even though he had the combination to the safe, it would not open—unless it was Friday at 4:00 p.m.

Eventually, he got clean. Whether he kept the safe I don't know.

You also don't have to lose everything, or hit "rock bottom," to qualify as an alcoholic or addict. When I was new, I sat down at an AA meeting and the old-timers laughed at me.

"You're wearing a watch," they helpfully pointed out. "In the old days, they would never have let you into a meeting wearing a watch. They would have said that you hadn't lost everything, so you needed to wait until you had lost everything before they would let you in."

You can still have the house on the hill, the spouse and the 2.4 children, two cars in the garage, and a promising future at work . . . and yet be an alcoholic or addict.

Don't let your own fancy clothes fool you.

It's harder to stop when you've got the world on a string. Why should you stop? Alcohol and other drugs don't seem to be holding you back.

But what kind of behavior are you modeling for your kids? What are you going to do when they simultaneously rebel against you and emulate you by getting drunk or high in a manner most likely different from yours? You like gin; they'll do lines of coke. You smoke grass; they'll drink beer. What are you going to tell them, do as I say and not as I do?

How are the alcohol and other drugs helping your marriage? Do they improve communication, aside from loosening your tongue?

How does it feel to go to work on those hungover, bloodshot mornings when lifting your head off the pillow feels like you're cracking a thin sheet of plate glass as you greet the new day? Does your boss like you better on days when you come in glassy-eyed or wearing a dark pair of sunglasses?

How effective are you after lunch, when all you had was a "beer or two"?

By the way, how can you tell when alcoholics or addicts are lying about how much booze and drugs they consumed?

Answer: their lips are moving.

Maybe you're telling yourself you're a functioning alcoholic. That you only use socially, or as a reward to yourself. But if you listen carefully, you're also telling yourself that you're an addict or alcoholic.

Most addicts don't want to be addicts. Most alcoholics don't want to be alcoholics. We want to be able to drink and use as we see fit.

We often trust alcohol and other drugs far more than we trust people, even those people we ostensibly love.

In our minds, drugs and alcohol aren't the problem. They're the solution.

In case of emergency, drink. Use. Find someone for sex. All your problems go away. Well, they might for the moment, but they'll still be there in the morning.

Another reason why alcoholics and addicts don't *want* to be alcoholics and addicts is because they often see it as shameful.

And they know many people think an alcoholic or an addict is a bad person. Nobody wants to think of himself or herself as being bad.

And yet, when we drink and use, we may not be bad people, but we certainly do a lot of bad things.

One of the best things Twelve Step programs have done is to remove the moral issue from drinking and using. We understand in the fellowship, as we've discussed, that addiction is a medical problem, not a moral issue.

We're not bad people getting good; we're sick people getting well.

Addicts and alcoholics often don't want to own up to their addictions because they know what lies ahead—giving up their best, most trusted friend. Going to those dreary meetings with those boring, self-righteous people.

Just shoot me.

It's your choice. I've never met you. My life will go on just fine whether you declare yourself to be an alcoholic or an addict, or just sidestep the whole issue.

But will you be everything that you could have been? The man or woman created to make a difference in the world? To serve others? To contribute? Or will you die a taker?

This is the stark choice that alcoholics and addicts face. In the fifth chapter of the Big Book, it says, "We stood at the turning point." Or as it's said in meetings, only an alcoholic or addict can stand at the intersection of happy, joyous, and free in one direction, and insanity, institutions, and death in the other, and stroke his chin.

Some people stay stuck on Step One for years. Why? Maybe they don't believe that something better than a life with drugs and alcohol is possible.

Maybe they've been to a Twelve Step program, and they didn't like it. Someone might have been mean to them.

Maybe contemplating life without an instant way of killing pain is too much to bear.

It's been said that Twelve Step programs do for you slowly what alcohol and other drugs did quickly.

Or as it says at the beginning of the 12&12, "Who cares to admit complete defeat?" That's what we mean by *powerless*. It means we're cooked. Out of gas. Done. ■

Q. What's the Deal with *Surrender*?

A. One of the most important words in Twelve Step recovery is *surrender*. Alcoholics and addicts begin to take Step One when they surrender to the reality that alcohol and other drugs are not safe or appropriate for them.

That moderation is not a concept to which immoderate people like us can relate.

Like I said, my sponsor warns, "Alcoholics [and presumably all addicts] don't taper off—they taper on."

Addicts may wish to postpone surrender for as long as they can, perhaps forever. But in reality, we are always surrendering. We are surrendering to the lower parts of our nature by giving in to the urge to drink and use.

If we drink or use in public, we may be surrendering to law enforcement.

The woman my Uber driver mentioned, sleeping alone on a bench in the middle of a city, might have been forced to surrender to an attacker. Things happen.

So as long as we're going to surrender anyway, why not make it a surrender that actually makes sense?

In war, surrender just means joining the winning side.

There was a guy at my first home group who used to say, "If you're a boozer, you're a loser."

I won't lie—I miss drinking. Twenty-four years into my sobriety, I still miss the burn of the first step of a fine unblended scotch. I was a Glenfiddich man, if you're curious.

I miss the foam mustache you get from the first sip of Guinness and the instant sense of release the alcohol provided.

I miss bringing two bottles of wine—one red and one white—to the restaurant with my date, because we weren't sure what we were going to order, meat or fish, and then drinking both bottles.

I miss squirting wine into my mouth at six in the morning at the Running of the Bulls festival in Pamplona, Spain.

I miss being seventeen and drinking scotch and water with my great-uncle. But I don't miss any of it enough to go back.

Joe and Charlie of "The Big Book Comes Alive" put it beautifully. They said sobriety is like chocolate pie. You can look at the recipe for chocolate pie, you could actually make a chocolate pie, but if you've never tasted chocolate pie, you'd have no idea how good it is.

And that's how I feel about my sobriety.

I like the fact that I can look the world, and my wife and children, in the eye. I like not blacking out anymore.

I like not waking up after having thrown up on myself the night before, fortunate not to have choked on my own vomit.

Did I mention that one morning I went to work in the clothing I had worn the night before, unaware that there was still dried vomit on my pants?

I like knowing that I can go out to dinner with people and that I'm not going to tell anyone that her daughter is ugly.

I like the fact that I am well liked in Alcoholics Anonymous. I'm not everyone's cup of tea, because I am rather serious about recovery, as you might guess. But I enjoy the long-term friendships I've developed over the course of my recovery.

I like the fact that I was able to choose substitute father figures through my sponsors, who gave me the love and healthy parenting that my own father was not capable of providing once his own drinking kicked in.

I like the fact that I'm accountable at work—that I run a successful business. That I'm respected in my field. That I have a reputation for honesty, trustworthiness, and doing a good job for people.

I like the fact that I have employees who've been with me for five, ten, twelve years.

I like the fact—and this may be too much information—that when I had to get my liver function tested so I could take an antifungal medication, my liver was just fine, thank you.

Looking back at things I've done, and situations I've been in, I am grateful for the fact that I didn't get hepatitis C from a dirty needle and that there's no chance of that happening today.

Maybe tomorrow, but not today.

I know a few people who had hepatitis C, were treated for it, and recovered. They may be the most grateful people in recovery I've ever met.

I like the fact that people are happy to see me arrive—in the old days, they were happier to see me go.

What was the price of all that success, self-worth, contribution, and peace of mind? I can't drink.

Better still, today, I don't have to drink.

The world will stop calling you an alcoholic or addict . . . only when you can call yourself one.

All you have to do is not drink today . . . and then tomorrow you get a fresh, new day, and you won't be hungover. Nice, huh?

Powerless doesn't mean weakness. It just means accepting a limitation and experimenting with life absent alcohol and other drugs.

Surrender ultimately means joining the winning side. There's plenty of room. Welcome aboard. ▪

A. Our lives became "unmanageable"—that's the second half of the First Step. *Unmanageable* means out of control. Alcoholics and addicts love to control everything. We love to control other people.

We love to control outcomes. We love to control situations. We love to control conversations. Why? Because control makes us feel safe.

Many alcoholics and addicts, myself included, grew up in homes where alcoholism and addiction reigned. As a result, we felt out of control in those places, because we never knew what was going to happen next. People from such homes often develop what's called hypermnesia—the opposite of amnesia.

Hypermnesia means you notice everything, most likely because you've been through trauma. You are much more aware than the average person of your surroundings. This probably happened at a young age when your life depended on your ability to assess, in the blink of an eye, whether your alcoholic or addicted parent was going to be violent, verbally or physically abusive, or mellow. If you were on guard as a child, you'll be on guard for the rest of your life.

I remember more than twenty years ago speaking at a veterans' shelter on Court Street in Boston. This was the early 1990s, and most of the men there had fought in the Vietnam War. They would often arrange their cots in to the same formations in which they had slept in Vietnam, with one man staying awake to "walk point." This made them feel safe.

So alcoholics and addicts feel most safe when they have a sense of control, no matter how illusory that control might be. Drinking and using is an effective way to control one's mood, surroundings, and interactions with others. I cannot change you, as hard as I might try, but I can certainly change the way I feel. I can do it with a beer, a bong, or a bag of M&Ms.

Ironically, the one thing alcoholics and addicts crave the most—control—is the very thing they surrender by continuing to drink and use.

When you pick up, you don't know where you'll end up.

It could be good—in an attractive stranger's bed (tough to explain to a spouse, but who am I to judge?).

It could be neutral—you weave your way back home.

A cop pulls over an eighty-two-year-old man who's weaving on the highway at two a.m. "Where do you think you're headed?" the cop asks.

"Headed to a lecture on the evils of drinking, smoking, and staying out too late," the old man replies.

"And who's going to deliver a lecture like that at two in the morning?" asks the cop.

"My wife," says the man.*

Or the outcome could be bad—we might find ourselves kicked out of the big bed and sleeping on the couch, or we might find ourselves, like those friends of mine, behind bars.

By using, we're spinning the giant roulette wheel of life, and we don't know what's going to happen. At the same time, we have an illusion of control over it. And we like that.

Unfortunately, as time goes on, we pay a price. We begin to lose the things that matter most to us.

Self-respect. Dignity. Employment. Relationships. Children. Our immortal souls, if you are so inclined.

---

*Couldn't resist.

I have yet to meet someone whose life was actually enhanced by decades of drinking and using.

Again, I'm not suggesting that bad things happen every time you pick up. That's not a precondition for needing sobriety.

I am saying that cumulatively, the trend is not your friend. You go from liking your drug of choice to craving it to being unable to live without it to giving up anything and everything just so you can get more.

You don't have to lose everything. You don't have to hit the lowest possible bottom. You don't have to be locked in the bathroom with the barrel of your gun in your mouth to say you've had enough. It just comes down to the question of what price you're willing to pay to keep on defending your right to drink and use.

Some people just don't expect much from life. They don't expect to see twenty, or thirty, or forty, or whatever birthday odometer lies ahead.

They don't expect to have a successful relationship, maybe because they've never seen one close up.

They don't expect to succeed financially, because everyone they've ever known is too broke to pay attention.

Others may have been exposed to the glittering prizes in life—a fine education, a great career, a nice home in an attractive neighborhood, the white picket fence, and the spouse or partner; add kids if so desired.

They just don't think they deserve it.

Or as a character on *Modern Family* said, "I eat garbage because I am garbage."

I'm here to tell you that God doesn't create junk, that God has no grandchildren, that God has your picture on his refrigerator.*

---

*As I once heard a young man say in a recovery house, "I call my Higher Power God, because that's his name."

One of the best things about AA, and other programs, is that you will encounter highly successful people who otherwise would have never encountered you. When my sister got sober, she was a typist for one of the top publishing companies. One of the people who attended her regular morning AA meeting was the CEO of that same company.

You'll meet people who have what you want, who have things you've never dreamt of, and who have things that, at this moment, you do not deserve.

Love. Security. A nice car. I remember how excited I was in early sobriety when I realized my car's license plates, my driver's license, my car insurance, and my home address were finally all the same thing.

Today I'd be tweeting about it. #Adulting.*

In Twelve Step meetings, you could be sitting in a meeting with a millionaire turned into a homeless person on one side and a homeless person turned into a millionaire on your other side.

In Los Angeles, you'll meet movie stars.

In New Bedford, Massachusetts, you'll meet fishermen.

You'll meet people who went to Yale and people who went to jail, and you'll meet people who went to Yale *and* jail.

The main thing is that you'll meet people who have gotten some semblance of control back in their lives.

Let me be clear. We in Twelve Step recovery do not have a magical elixir for finally controlling everyone else.

In fact, we advise the opposite—we believe in "Live and let live." What we get is control over our words and our actions.

---

*This hashtag refers to the mistaken idea that you are acting like an adult if you pay your phone bill on time or do your laundry without taking it home to Mom. Not so. Being an adult means taking on real life responsibilities—entering into a relationship with a no-exit clause tattooed on your brain; committing to a career. Committing to *yourself*. It's such a big topic you could write a whole book about it. And I did just that. Look for it from your friends at Hazelden Publishing.

These are the only two things that we can possibly control.

You cannot control other people—and that includes your children, your spouse, your partner, and anyone else with free will.

You cannot control outcomes—how much money you will make, whether you'll get the job or keep the job, whether your business will be successful or not.

But by having control restored to you with regard to the only two things you can control—your words and your actions—your life will get immeasurably better.

If you're honest, you'll have a better life.

If you're hardworking, you'll make more money.

So the second half of the First Step, "that our lives had become unmanageable," asks us to acknowledge that our lives, when we drink or use, are in fact out of control. We lose and we lose and we lose.

Inevitably, beneath every bottom is a trap door. I once heard in a meeting that if you pick up (get high or drunk), within a few days you'll feel nostalgic for how miserable you felt the moment before you picked up. In other words, things are going to get worse. Never better.

If you're trying to control your drinking and using, that's a strong hint that your drinking and using are already out of control.

The second half of Step One asks us to stop the futile quest to control the uncontrollable. Instead, we just admit—Step One requires an admission, nothing more—that our lives are not what we want them to be.

We aren't managing them well.

We may be trying to control things, but we aren't getting anything like the results we desire.

If you are willing to admit that your life is not what you want it to be—that your relationships, financial life, career, housing situation, relationships with family members, physical health—if you can acknowledge that these things are out of control in a meaningful way (and the definition of meaningful is up to you and you alone), then you are buying into the second half of Step One.

It takes an admission of unmanageability in order to succeed in Twelve Step recovery, because people who still think they're all that and a bag of chips are just not ready to do what it takes to get sober.

So now we've seen the two halves of the First Step—powerlessness and unmanageability. If you can admit to both, then you're ready to take the First Step. Let's do that right now. How to do it is the subject of the next question. ■

Q. So, How Do I Take Step One?

A. You've seen the first and second halves of the First Step—an admission of powerlessness over alcohol, drugs, or whatever, and then, on the other side of the dash, an acknowledgment of unmanageability or a sense that things were out of control.

What's the dash for?

The dash comes along to tell us that we need to see a connection between these two phenomena—powerlessness and unmanageability.

In other words, can you see the connection between the fact that your life is out of control in one or more key departments and the fact that you drink and use? That's the dilemma. Taking Step One is really simple. Maybe not easy, but simple. Once you can acknowledge the connection between powerlessness over substances or unhealthy behaviors on the one hand and the fact that your life is out of control on the other, you've taken Step One.

Sometimes getting to this point takes months or years. We're stubborn people.

Sometimes we've been so beaten down by alcohol, drugs, or other addictive substances and behaviors that we agree to the idea in Step One the moment we hear it.

So now I'll ask you the Step One question: *Can you see the connection between powerlessness and the unmanageability of your life when you drink or use?*

If so, congratulations. You've taken Step One. ■

Q. If I Don't Like Step Two, Do I Still Have to Take It?

A. A lot of people in recovery find Step Two insulting.

Not the whole Step. Just the last few words—the idea of being restored to sanity. There's a not-so-subtle implication that, well, we are insane.

But are we?

Sane just means healthy. Is there anything healthy about the way we drank, used, or behaved?

Anything?

Of course, many of us were never sane to begin with. I don't think I was.

I don't know if I was a born liar, but I certainly started lying at a young age. I would lie when I could just as easily tell the truth. I would lie when I had nothing to hide.

I started drinking in high school, but I didn't drink during the school year. I really only had easy access to alcohol in the summers, so that's when I drank, starting when I was thirteen years old.

My first drunk happened on a brewery tour with my father in Copenhagen the week after my fourteenth birthday. After you took the tour, you'd get all the beer you wanted.

Even a fourteen-year-old kid. Me.

Weren't the 1970s great?

Is it sane for a fourteen-year-old kid to be getting drunk with his father?

Or to get drunk every chance he could that summer and every summer that followed? Seemed like a good idea at the time.

So I understand the sense of insult that many people in recovery experience when they see the last few words of the Second Step.

"I'm not insane," they insist. Sure you aren't.

Did you drink in a healthy manner? Were you strictly a social heroin user? A social garbage can?*

Are you catching my drift?

For addicts and alcoholics, there is nothing healthy or sane about drinking or using. It's that simple.

Of course, as Joe and Charlie said, "It's just as hard to be restored to sanity if you've never been sane as it is to come back to a place you've never been to." Any questions? Good. Let's move on. Quickly.

The key phrase in the Second Step is "a Power greater than ourselves." Of the Twelve Steps, only one deals with the problem—the First Step. The next eleven are all oriented toward the solution. In Alcoholics Anonymous and every Twelve Step program of which I am aware, the solution is spiritual.

As we've discussed earlier, you don't have to call that Power "God." You don't have to call it by any name that anyone else chooses.

The Power you choose to keep you sober doesn't depend on the name you give it for its strength. Any term we use, whether it's God, the universe, the Great Spirit, or whatever, is simply a shorthand way of thinking about something that we cannot possibly understand.

If I cut my finger with a knife, instantly my body will start to heal. I don't know how. If I don't understand how my finger can heal itself, how on earth can I possibly understand—fully comprehend—the concept of God?

---

*A garbage can is a self-described consumer of any pill or drug, regardless of source, potency, or purpose.

But at the same time, as my sponsor says, who knows more about God than you do?

Not the theologians or religious leaders. Their guesses are as good as yours. And your Higher Power is just as powerful as theirs.

The Step doesn't say "came to a Twelve Step program and instantly believed that God, or some God substitute, could get me to stop drinking and using and could make my life really swell."

The words it uses are "came to believe."

For most people, the process of recognizing the existence of a Power greater than ourselves is time-consuming. *Universe* seems so impersonal. People live and die without understanding why they were born. We hurtle through space on a large rock, governed by little more than the laws of physics and the Internal Revenue Service.

We understand next to nothing.

It's a leap to go from the idea that "my finger knows how to heal itself when it gets a cut" to "there's a Power that can arrest my addiction." But that's the leap that we all make.

Even people who come to Twelve Step fellowships with a strong background in the church or the synagogue or the mosque can struggle with the idea of believing that God, so high and mighty, to whom great songs are sung, for whom incense is burned, could give a rap about their alcoholism or drug use.

That's why the Step says *came to believe* as opposed to suddenly believed.

If you suddenly believe, great. You'll have an easier time than the rest of us. But for most people, came to believe means this:

Came. Started showing up at Twelve Step meetings with the recognition that maybe there was something here for me.

Came to. Recognized that I am living life in an unconscious, reflexive manner, without any regard for what drinking and using was doing to me or to the people around me.

Came to believe. Finally, over time, after having witnessed and absorbed the testimony of countless clean and sober members of AA, NA, or whatever A.

Came to believe, in my own time and in my own way, that a Power greater than myself, which I get to define, without having to take on the beliefs of anyone else, could restore me to sanity— could restore in me the power of choice with regard to drinking or using.

One of the greatest casualties of addiction is the power of choice. Do you wake up in the morning and say, "I'm not going to drink, or use, or eat ice cream, or have sex with a stranger today!"? And then, somehow, you end up "beating on the bar," in Bill W.'s felicitous Big Book phrase, or the bedpost, or, to paraphrase the existential philosopher Britney Spears, oops, you've done it again.

Or you're only going to have one or two, but instead you had ten or twenty? More than once you'd started to feel you could stop?

Hello!

The Big Book suggests that we consider our program a "Power greater than ourselves." In AA, we find countless individuals who have been able to do something you cannot—namely, stay sober, a day at a time, day after day, year after year. If you want to make your Twelve Step program your Higher Power, you won't be the first, and it will work.

Are you allowed to modify your concept of your Higher Power as time goes on? Of course. One of the beautiful things about Twelve Step recovery is that there is no rigidity in this regard.

The only thing you have to do perfectly, and the same way as everybody else, is not drink or use. After that, it's up to you.

When I was newly sober, my first sponsor had me read the chapter of the Big Book called "We Agnostics" every morning for a month.

"You're agnostic about your alcoholism," he said.

He was right. *Agnostic* simply means that you don't know. I didn't really know if I was an alcoholic, and I didn't really know if anything could help me if I were. Reading that chapter, day after day, helped a lot. I was particularly struck by Bill's assertion that life, as complex as it is, could have no meaning. Ultimately, things get binary, he wrote—either there is a God or there isn't. And ultimately, who am I to say there is no God?

He was right. At least he was right for me. Who exactly am I to say that there is no God? It would be a little like my finger saying there was no me.

How would it know?

In "We Agnostics," Bill also made the point that those of us who are afraid to worship God have always worshipped something. We've looked out at a starlit night and asked who created all this, or we looked at the miracle of birth and we wondered how this phenomenon came to be. (Then, if you're a parent, you start wondering when that phenomenon will brush and floss without you standing over him, but that's a subject for another day.)*

You've always worshipped something, Bill wrote. Maybe we didn't like the religious services we might have been forced to attend as children. Maybe the religious leaders in our community were less than stellar human beings. But if you strip all that away, Bill wrote, you end up with "the fundamental idea of God," which he believed could be found in every human being.

You may hate God, as I did, for the things that happened previously in our lives. We may be afraid of God, or ashamed of ourselves before God. But that Higher Power can always be found, and as Bill wrote, can be found within.

---

*Or better still, a subject for another book. How about *Sober Dad*? It's a book I wrote about parenting, and I am shamelessly marketing it for you here. Published by Hazelden Publishing and available on Amazon and at the better bookstores, assuming you can still find a bookstore.

Came to believe that a Power greater than ourselves could restore us to sanity.

That's a complicated way of saying that "the same way that my body has a God-given ability to heal a cut without my conscious intervention, there exists within me an even greater power or force I do not understand. And that Power can handle my addiction problem in ways that I can never understand, nor do I ever need to understand."

Alcoholics and addicts are driven, Bill wrote, by "a hundred forms of fear." Because we are fearful, we want to understand how things work. Because we're fearful about substituting the unknown experience of a sober life for drugs and alcohol, we want to understand exactly how the process works.

Unfortunately, no one really knows.

The biggest clue can be found toward the back of the Big Book, where sobriety is defined as a combination of survival instinct plus the herd instinct. In Twelve Step recovery, you've got a whole group of people who are all running in the same direction—they want to get well. It's hard to buck the herd when you're in the middle of it.

Do you like Step Two a little bit more now that I've broken it down this way? Does it make sense, and could you find yourself buying into the idea, no matter how absurd it may seem at first?

If so, then I have very exciting news.

If you can accept the idea that something can help you, that something, whether it's outside you or inside you, nameable or unnameable, knowable or unknowable, can restore to you the power of choice with regard to alcohol or other drugs, so you can say on any given morning that you're not going to indulge, and then you don't, day after day—and that's as good a definition of sanity as an addict could hope to find—then you've taken Step Two.

Taking the Step doesn't mean that you are letting God take over. It just means that you're open to the idea that something can help you. Whether it's God, a Group Of Drunks, or anything else under (or over) the sun.

In Step One, you acknowledged that there was a connection between how out of control your life has become and the fact that you cannot drink or use safely.

You've defined the problem.

Now in Step Two, you've acknowledged the idea that something can help you. That there is a spiritual solution to the problem you defined in Step One.

You're now *living* in the solution. Congratulations—you've now taken Steps One and Two. ▩

Q. What's Step Three?

A. In the first two Steps, we acknowledged the problem—that we cannot safely drink because our lives go out of control when we drink or use—and the solution, that a Power greater than ourselves can solve the problem.

In Step Three, we simply ask that Power to handle the situation for us.

In other words, Step Three is a decision to let the Power of which we have become aware, and which we now believe can help us, to go ahead and help us. I could overcomplicate it for you, but that's what the whole concept boils down to: asking for spiritual help.

You can see why Dr. Bob might have been frustrated with Bill W. for creating three Steps—whose language was somewhere between tortuous and inexplicable on its face—when he could say the same thing with just one Step.

For Bob, the three concepts of problem, solution, and decision to apply the solution, were really just one big idea.

Members of Twelve Step programs also simplify the first three Steps into a simple, practical formula. "I can't, God can, I'll let God."

So how exactly do you do that?

There's no one right way. The simplest thing is to just say out loud, "I'm deciding to let God solve the problem."

Done.

If you're a traditionalist, you can take the Third Step on your knees while reciting the Third Step Prayer, which is found on page 63 of the fourth edition of the Big Book.

If you want to really enjoy the full benefits of the Third Step, then let's go more deeply into the language and seek to understand exactly what Bill had in mind. So, let's look at that language. "Made a decision to turn our will and our lives over to the care of God *as we understood Him.*"

Made a decision—that's straightforward. The verb *decide* means to cut. So *to decide* means to cut ourselves off from all other options. Making a decision, therefore, means that we have cut ourselves off from anything other than what the rest of the Step says: to turn *our will and our lives* over to the care of God.

Our *what* and our *what*?

I'm not convinced that the language was any clearer when Bill wrote it in the late 1930s.

Once again, we look to Joe and Charlie for the explanation.

Your will, they explained, means your thinking. In order to illustrate the point in a memorable fashion, Joe spoke of what would happen when he died and his family ran to the lawyer's office to find out who got what. That would be determined by Joe's last will and testament.

In other words, your will is your thinking. So when we turn our will over to the care of God, we are actually asking God to direct our thoughts.

What comes next? Our lives. Joe explained that all of the actions that each of us has taken up to this point in our lives have resulted in the fact that we are exactly the way that we are right now. To put it simply, if you take better actions, you will get better results. So to turn our lives over to the care of God, or a Higher Power by any other name, means that we are asking God to direct our actions.

Put it together, and the Third Step asks us to decide to let God direct our thoughts and our actions.

This does not mean that you will suddenly become an automaton uniquely capable of hearing God's voice at all times and inevitably acting on the guidance and direction you receive. I was speaking about this with a newcomer not too long ago. He was afraid that if he took the Third Step, he would lose *agency*—the ability to make decisions for himself. In other words, he would lose his dignity as an adult.

I asked him to tell me about his most recent family vacation, and how much dignity he maintained on the days when he was drinking.

Newcomers hate it when you do that.

Just because you're asking God to direct your thoughts and your actions does not mean you become a marionette with strings extending heavenward. Instead, you suddenly have a choice of thoughts and actions. In my case, it's a choice to move away from the selfish, rather thoughtless thoughts and actions I had back in the day, such as the brilliant idea to tell my fiancée's mother about how ugly my beloved looked in a photo when she was a first-grader.

Had I made a Third Step that morning, I would very likely have heard another voice in my head: Don't say that she looked ugly. It will only hurt people's feelings.

And instead I would have said, "She's so cute."

And perhaps I would now be celebrating thirty years of wedded bliss with that woman, instead of having alienated her and crushed her feelings (and her mother's feelings).

So it isn't as though you're subjecting yourself to some sort of spiritual mind control when you take the Third Step. Instead, you *get* choices. You actually develop the ability to remain silent instead of saying the thing that would only cause heartache and require an amend later on. Instead of feeling that you have no choice but to pick up and use, the power of choice has been restored to you, with regard to the act of drinking and using, and with regard to everything else in your life.

It's almost as though you've downloaded new software for running your brain. Sober software. You 2.0. You still have the choice of saying or doing stupid things. It's just that you don't *have* to do them anymore.

Doesn't that sound great?

I had a very hard time believing that my Higher Power cared enough about me, or about any human being, to respond to a request for directing thoughts and actions. I figured God was too busy, too distracted, or just not interested enough in me. Yet after taking the Third Step, I found to my surprise that over and over again, I was saying nice things instead of mean things and doing kind things instead of selfish things.

I began to like myself better.

I gradually became less of a jerk.

All because I asked my Higher Power to direct my thoughts and my actions—all because, in the language of the Step, I turned my will and my life over to the care of God.

Again, it's not a crawl of faith. It is indeed a leap. To go from thinking that I was the master of my own universe to actually allowing another voice in, a voice that's actually wiser and healthier than the way my mind worked—was very exciting. Very satisfying. Again, as my sponsor says, if you act like a decent person and talk like a decent person and show up like a decent person, people will begin to mistake you for a decent person. And that's exactly how it was for me and for the millions of others who have taken this Step.

If you'd like to take the Third Step, don't let me stand in your way. You'll immediately start hearing the voice of God ringing in your ears. My late grand-sponsor, Bob H., used to say that he never received a letter from God under his pillow every morning saying, "Dear Bob, here is my will for you today. Love, God."

Instead, it's just one of these things you have to experience for yourself. You can always take your will back at any given moment. You can always tell your Higher Power, "I'll handle this. I'll see you in a couple of hours. Maybe go have a cup of coffee while I go out and do the wrong thing." God is remarkably patient, at least in my experience. He's put up with a whole lot of nonsense from me, certainly.

The Big Book says, "The spiritual life is not a theory. *We have to live it.*" In other words, we have to take the first two Steps. We have to acknowledge the problem, and we have to acknowledge the solution. But an intellectual acknowledgment that the solution exists doesn't mean that we're actually living in it. Step Three is when we start to take on the spiritual life of the program for ourselves. ■

Q. What's the Contract in the Third Step?

A. Back in 1992, when I got sober, my sponsor told me that there was a contract in the Third Step. He also told me that not one person in fifty could find it, but that I was welcome to try.

By the way, though I no longer practice, I'm a former attorney with an Ivy League law school diploma hanging proudly in my storage room. I didn't find the contract. It took a lot of digging and asking around to uncover the contract's subtle language. To prevent you from having to do the work on your own, let's just find it together, shall we?

The contract can be found in the second half of the Third Step Prayer, which can be found on page 63 of the fourth edition of the Big Book. That sentence reads, "Take away my difficulties, that victory over them may bear witness to those I would help of Thy Power, Thy Love, and Thy Way of life."

This is where the contract could be found. So what's the deal?

First, let's determine who the parties are. This much I got right. A prayer is between a human being and his or her Higher Power, so the parties to this contract were my Higher Power and me.

So what did we each have to do, and why? God's part is revealed in the first four words of the sentence—*take away my difficulties*.

In other words, it's my job to tell God my difficulties, and his job to take them away. But what do I do? What can I do, as it were, for God?

May bear witness—bear witness just means testifying, or to put it more simply, talking about something.

To those I would help—fellow alcoholics or addicts.

Of Thy Power, Thy Love, and Thy Way of life—these are the things I'm supposed to talk about with other people in my fellowship.

Put it all together, and it works like this: God will keep on taking in my difficulties. In exchange for that, since I've found a spiritual path, it's up to me to *bear witness*, or talk, with *those I would help*—fellow members who are trying to find a spiritual path for themselves—*of Thy Power, Thy Love, and Thy Way of life*—in other words, my concept of a Higher Power so that they can see that they can create a concept of a Higher Power for themselves.

In even simpler terms, it means that if I am willing to let God take away my difficulties, and then if I'm willing to help others find their own Higher Power by describing what mine has done for me, then God will keep on taking away my difficulties. You've heard of the term *vicious cycle*? This is the opposite—a virtuous cycle, a gaining game.

"The hardest thing in the world for most alcoholics," my sponsor said, "is to create a relationship with a Higher Power. The most important thing you can talk about, whether one-on-one or when you're sharing in meetings, is how your Higher Power is helping you."

And that's what I've done to this day. Whenever I'm sitting in a meeting and thinking about what I want to share about, invariably this still, small voice inside speaks to me. It's my Higher Power, and the voice is saying, "Talk about me."

You know the expression "teach a man to fish"? Well, if you can teach a person in recovery about how to have a relationship with a Higher Power of his or her understanding, you will have taught that person to fish.

That's the contract that's in the Third Step—it's actually in the Third Step Prayer. Help others see how your Higher Power is taking away your difficulties, so that maybe they'll ask their Higher Power to do the same for them.

It's not a bad contract when you think about it. I've got a pen. Sign here. ▪

Q. How Do You Tell the Difference between My Will and God's Will?

A. The difference between my will and God's will is pain.

If I'm about to take an action, or say something, and that action or those words will cause myself or someone else pain, it's probably not God's will, is it?

The only asterisk on this is early sobriety itself, which is painful. Here you are, living without your best friend, Budweiser, cocaine, ice cream, a credit card, or Mr. or Ms. Right Now; pick your poison. When I came in, I was told it took eight months to get all the alcohol out of my bone marrow. When you're new, it seems as if everything in life is geared to make you want to drink or use.

Like the end of the workday (if you're fortunate enough to still be working). Or a beer ad on TV.

Or if a stranger looked at you funny.

Or somebody wouldn't have sex with you. Or somebody *would* have sex with you.

Suddenly you have to develop "sober references"—experiences in situations where you don't use or drink.

Maybe you got on a plane and got loaded. Now you have to learn to fly without alcohol or taking a pill. It's doable.

Maybe you never golfed without a six-pack in the cooler on the back of the golf cart. (Your score is likely to improve, because now you know which ball to hit.)

Maybe you've never had sex without chemical assistance. You might like it. You might like it more!

In chapter 5 of the Big Book, right after the Twelve Steps, Bill wrote of the "ABCs" of alcoholism: "(a) That we were alcoholic and could not manage our own lives. (b) That probably no human power could have relieved our alcoholism. (c) That God could and would if He were sought."

Well, this is how you seek God in Twelve Step recovery. You just put your hand up and ask for help. Or hit your knees. Or just talk to God while you're driving. Plenty of recovering people pray while they drive (and probably plenty more of their passengers pray, too!).

The Third Step is absolutely my favorite Step, because it gave me so much. By the time I was done drinking, I was done drinking. I do miss it, as I wrote, but not so much that I'd pine over bygone days at the bar. It's a phase of my life that's over. As Joe and Charlie said, we get to lead two lives—the sober one and the recovered one. Nice.

Speaking for myself, the benefit of having access to the spiritual guidance that pops up in my head, as wacky as that may sound, far outweighs whatever I went through while drinking. In other words, the rewards of the program are so much more dramatic than the losses incurred by giving up drinking and using. Your decision to take the Third Step may be the most important decision you've ever made.

Is it more important than stopping drinking and using? Perhaps, because lots of people, myself included, have stopped many times. The Third Step, in which we ask and receive spiritual help, is the beginning of the process by which we don't just stop—we stay stopped, a day at a time, forever. ■

A. It didn't happen overnight. Initially, I treated God like an office boy, giving him simple tasks to handle, hoping that he wouldn't mess them up too badly, so that I could trust him with something more important, namely my sobriety, my will, and my life.

One day, my friend Mike had come to visit me in Los Angeles, where I lived at the time,* and we were off to play golf. Suddenly, on Ventura Boulevard, my Toyota Camry rolled to a stop. Just completely gave up the ghost.

I looked up at the sky. "Okay, God, let's see what you can do."

We looked around, and there was a Range Rover dealership in the vicinity, so we walked there and explained our plight.

The mechanic we spoke with shrugged and said, "This is a Range Rover dealership, but we just hired a guy named Frank who was a Toyota-trained factory mechanic."

Toyota-trained factory mechanic? Hmm. Interesting, I thought to myself.

We went over to see Frank. I told him what had happened. "How many miles does your car have?" he asked.

"About 65,000," I said.

Frank nodded knowingly, as only car mechanics can. "It's the timing belt," he said authoritatively. "They go on Camrys at about

---

*As the expression goes, "Anyone who was ever told even once that they were good looking moves to L.A."

65,000 miles. I tell you what, I had the same problem with my car, so I bought two timing belts. I've got another one right here.

"You could take it to Toyota, and they would charge you $900. Or I could do it for you right here, and I'll just charge you $600."

I looked at Frank, looked at my friend, and then looked up at the heavens and addressed my Higher Power.

"God," I said, defeated, "quit showing off."

I gave Frank the keys. Five minutes later, Enterprise Rent-A-Car picked us up. We got the golf clubs out of the trunk of my car and were headed to the course, and we wouldn't even be late for our tee time. We still had time to play.

"That was amazing," my friend Mike said. I nodded.

"Either my Higher Power just came through for me in a wonderful and miraculous way," I said, "or I just gave my car to a guy named Frank."

That's when I came to believe.

P.S. Frank was the real deal. He was my mechanic for the rest of the time I owned that car. Okay, God. You got the promotion. ■

Q.

How Does the First Step Apply in Al-Anon?

A. First, let's make clear that Al-Anon is for individuals who are affected by the drinking or sobriety of a loved one, friend, work associate, or anyone alive or dead. AA members call Al-Anon "the graduate program" because it's where you learn to have relationships with other people. AA, NA, OA, and the like are about reshaping your relationship with a substance or behavior. Al-Anon is about living life in the real world with other folks.

It's said that every alcoholic affects at least ten other people, and that's probably an undercount.

When you think about all the family members, girlfriends or boyfriends, spouses and partners, ex-employers (because we always get fired), and other folks whose paths we cross, we alcoholics and addicts probably have a powerful influence on dozens of people. Given the fact that alcoholism is so pervasive in our society, and the fact that so many alcoholics and addicts come from alcoholic homes, it makes sense for us to pause and discuss the message (and benefits) of working an Al-Anon program as well.

Since that's the case, and Al-Anon is intended to serve those who have been affected by alcoholics, drinking or sober, alive or dead, it stands to reason that Al-Anon meetings ought to be ten to twenty times the size of AA meetings.

And yet the reverse is true. Why?

Because although the Big Book describes alcohol as a "subtle foe," the outward manifestations of alcoholism are vivid, florid, and hard to hide.

Getting fired. Drunk driving. Accidents. Arrests. Infidelity. Domestic violence. It's hard not to notice the signs of alcoholism.

It's much more subtle and difficult to discern the effects of alcoholics on other people. Alcoholism is a disease; the Al-Anon state of mind is a condition. You may hear "Al-Anonism" described incorrectly as a disease in Al-Anon meetings, but that's not the case. So what does it mean exactly to be an Al-Anon?

It means that you have every aspect of alcoholism—the personality traits of the alcoholic—minus the compulsion to drink.

I'll repeat that because it's so startling—the alcoholic personality is so strong that it actually transforms the personalities of the people around the alcoholic, such that those other individuals, be they family members, friends, or others whose lives are closely entwined with the alcoholic, take on the same characteristics as the practicing alcoholic.

It's hard to imagine that that's the case, but that's what happens. An untreated Al-Anon has the same cluster of character defects as the untreated alcoholic.

This is actually good news, because it's been discovered, over the years, that the same solution—the Twelve Steps—that creates recovery from alcoholism also creates recovery for Al-Anons. In other words, if an Al-Anon follows the Twelve Steps, he or she will have the same spiritual awakening, and the same better life, as the alcoholic gets in AA—whether the alcoholic is still drinking or not.

The joke, and it's not that funny a joke, is that when Al-Anons have near-death experiences, they see the alcoholics' lives passing before their eyes.

In this sense, an Al-Anon is someone who is addicted to the experience of being around alcoholics.

A boy raised by an alcoholic mother grows up to be interested primarily in alcoholic women.

A girl with an alcoholic father only wants to get involved with alcoholic men.

Al-Anon is often described as an addiction to people, or as they used to say in the program, "Our drink has two legs."

Recovery in Al-Anon, therefore, means surrendering the addiction to people—especially those people who are incapable of providing the kind of love and support that an individual deserves. The Big Book says, "An alcoholic in his cups is an unlovely creature." *Unlovely* is the perfect word—his behavior is unlovable, and he is incapable of loving. To bounce from one pain-filled relationship to the next, or to oscillate between a painful relationship and painful loneliness, is no fun.[2] It's in the best interests of the Al-Anon to get off that cycle.

I'm not speaking theoretically. Al-Anon was my first Twelve Step program. I joined the Al-Anon fellowship on August 25, 1987, which means I've been around for a few twenty-four hours. I worked the Steps in Al-Anon, was sponsored and sponsored others in that fellowship, and have nothing but respect for it. Alcoholics and addicts who disrespect the Al-Anon fellowship and Al-Anons in general are missing out on an important aspect of life.

It's a form of defensiveness. It's a form of hostility. Ultimately, it's just childish behavior. For recovering alcoholics and addicts, Al-Anon is truly the graduate program, the place you go to learn how to have a relationship with yourself and other people. It's the place to repair the damage done growing up in an alcoholic or addicted home, and it's a place to learn how to stop inflicting damage on others in relationships.

So what does it mean to take Step One in Al-Anon? Since Al-Anon is not a forum for getting sober, it serves a different purpose. Although the language of Step One remains the same, the meaning is different. In Al-Anon, the precise meaning of Step One is that one acknowledges powerlessness *over the effects of alcohol on other people.*

That's so important I'll repeat it. In Al-Anon, the language of the First Step remains the same, but the meaning is different.

The meaning is that we admit powerlessness *over the effects of alcohol on other people.*

In other words, it takes courage to admit that my love is not enough to get you to stop drinking.

Anybody who tells you that love conquers all has never been to Al-Anon, because there you learn that love doesn't conquer all. It conquers a lot, but love is no match for active addiction.

Speaking of addiction, can addicts who don't define themselves as alcoholics become members of the Al-Anon fellowship? Chances are, the sap in the family tree of an addict is at least ninety proof. In other words, there's an awfully good chance that someone in the life of an addict is or was alcoholic—a parent, a sibling, a child. Someone, somewhere in the past or present qualifies most addicts for Al-Anon.

Here's an interesting sideline. About twenty-five years ago, my Al-Anon sponsor actually got a change made in my favorite piece of Al-Anon literature, the dos and don'ts. If you've never read the dos and don'ts,[3] it's the greatest. If all you followed in life were the Al-Anon dos and don'ts, you would be working a fabulous program, and you would be an even more fabulous person than you already are. Find this list online or get a copy at an Al-Anon meeting, read it, and live it.

When the dos and don'ts were first written, the suggestion "don't keep checking up on the alcoholic" appeared as "don't keep checking up on your alcoholic." The implication of the prior version was that the Al-Anon had some sort of possessory interest in the alcoholic—that he or she owned the alcoholic in some sense, and therefore had a right to do as he or she felt.

My sponsor very patiently took the issue up the Al-Anon chain of command, as it were. The issue came up for a vote, and the change was made. The dos and don'ts now reflect the fact that the alcoholic does not belong to the person in Al-Anon. The alcoholic belongs to God. The person working his or her program in Al-Anon is now admonished not to check up on *the* alcoholic instead of *his or her* alcoholic. It's a subtle change, but it's an important one.

Here's a business model I came up with when I was fairly new in Al-Anon. I never got around to starting this business, but if you're looking for a way to make easy money, feel free to run with it.

The company is called Rent-A-Drunk. It works this way: Practicing alcoholics are driven all over the city in town cars. You can order one. Back then, you would have had to call an 800 number, but today you can just use the Rent-A-Drunk app on your smartphone. The alcoholic arrives in a state of mild intoxication. For as long as you wish, you can reason with the alcoholic and try to get him (it probably works best if the alcoholics are male) to stop drinking. You can bribe him. You can make him promises. You can get him to sign a contract to quit drinking. And then when you've had enough, you just return the alcoholic through the convenient drop slot at Rent-A-Drunk headquarters.

I think you could make a fortune.

The serious point is that it's extremely hard to get people to recognize that they are powerless over their addiction. It's ten times harder to get people to recognize that their lives are negatively affected by the presence, now or in the past, of an alcoholic in their lives. It's a tough sell. It takes enormous courage to go into Al-Anon, because no one wants to admit that (a) his or her love is not enough to get the alcoholic to stop drinking, and (b) that one's own personality was essentially warped by close contact with another person. It seems undignified somehow. I found enormous relief, recovery, and even serenity in the Al-Anon program. Whether you are an hour sober or you're an old-timer, I cannot say enough good about Al-Anon, and I urge you to give the program a try.

You might suggest that your loved ones give it a shot also. When two people in a relationship are working a program, things can get better faster. ▪

PART 3

Questions People Often Ask in Early Twelve Step Recovery

Okay, so now you've taken the first
three Steps (or at least you read about them
and you found them vaguely interesting).
Here are answers to some questions that
you might be wondering about.

Q. What if I'm Taking Medication for Depression, Anxiety, or Other Issues?

A. If I could change one thing in Twelve Step programs,* it would be to ban people who are not qualified from telling other people whether or not they should get off their meds.

It never ceases to amaze me how individuals who, just a few short years ago, were too drunk or stoned to pull up their own fly, suddenly feel that they are as qualified to speak about medication as if they were Harvard-trained psychopharmacologists.

I've seen bad results when individuals, whether well meaning, power-tripping, or both, told newcomers that medication prescribed by doctors or psychiatrists somehow violated the tenets of the program. How would they know? Why are they saying these things? Do they have a brain in their heads?

I have no idea whether taking Ambien to help you sleep, if it's been prescribed by a doctor, is a violation of one's sobriety. Therefore, I don't give advice about it. It's an outside issue on which I have no experience, and therefore, I keep my mouth shut. Why can't all of us do that? It takes a little bit of humility to admit that you don't know something. When it comes to untrained, unqualified addicts and alcoholics who feel comfortable about giving advice on medication to others, especially newcomers, humility appears to be in short supply.

So if you're new, it's best that you don't share at group level about whatever you're taking. First of all, nobody cares, but even

---

*That whole business about "acceptance" is so annoying.

if they do care, it's none of their beeswax. Second of all, it's not going to help someone else get or stay sober, and if it won't do that, then it's probably not germane to the meeting. And third, the last thing you need is some unqualified drunk or addict influencing a decision that should best be made by you and your physician.

I have spoken. ■

Why Is Everyone in Twelve Step Programs So Damned Grateful?

A. Newcomers can't stand gratitude. I get it. Your life feels so jacked, and here are all these sparkly, happy people expressing great gratitude for everything that happened in their lives. They got a parking space! Somebody took pity on them and had (sober) sex with them! They found a shiny penny in the street! I am so grateful! This kind of enthusiasm makes it necessary to have a strong gag reflex if you're going to make a successful start in Twelve Step recovery.

And yes. Gratitude is one of the cornerstones of the program.

It's especially shocking to newcomers that people would express gratitude for being an alcoholic or addict. Many of us feel, however, that our addiction or alcoholism, and all the trouble we went through while using or drinking, turns out to have been a small price to pay for all the benefits that sobriety provides. We have a fellowship around us. We have a relationship with a Higher Power. We have a purpose for our lives that we might have lacked.

We are all about love and service. Life makes sense. And if your life never made sense before, why, that's one more thing for which to be grateful.

It's said that a grateful heart doesn't drink or use. And it's true. Whatever you focus on, grows. If you focus on all the negatives in your life, you will talk yourself into slipping. Poor me, poor me, pour me a drink. Or hand me a bong. On the other hand, if you focus on what you're grateful for, you'll feel better. Even if it's something as small as a parking space or that shiny penny, sobriety could be said to hinge on developing an attitude of gratitude.

If you've been drinking, snorting, or whatevering for a long time with disastrous results, and suddenly you're able to make it through even a single day clean and sober, aren't you grateful for that? We are. And if you aren't grateful for that, if you miss your drink or drug of choice, eventually you'll become grateful.

My first sponsor told me that when things were going wrong in my life, I was to use even those moments as opportunities to get closer to my Higher Power. I was to say, "Thank you, God, for the pain! Thank you, God, for the fear! Thank you, God, for the anxiety!"

It sounds crazy, but it worked.

One of the smartest things you can do is buy yourself a little notebook, carry it around, and every day write down at least three things for which you are grateful, no matter how big or how small. Cultivate the attitude of gratitude. It's one of the shortcuts to contented sobriety.

Wait a minute . . . phone's ringing . . . be right back . . . ■

Q. Hey, Michael, Who Was on the Phone Just Now?

A. Wow! Just now, as I was writing the previous section, guess what happened? That's right—the phone rang. It wasn't a sponsee. It was a member of the AA program with eleven months of sobriety who wanted to talk about a situation in his home, where he lives with his girlfriend and her son. An event upset him and his first thought was to use. Instead, he called his sponsor and left a voicemail, and then he called me.

How happy am I? I got to do exactly what I was talking about a moment earlier—be of service, be useful, carry the message, and enhance my own program. Ain't life grand?

One of the things we discussed was a point I learned in Al-Anon that I found life-changing: I cannot help anyone I'm emotionally involved with. I cannot "fix." I cannot control.

That's so important, I'll repeat it. I cannot help anyone I'm emotionally involved with. I can give him encouragement. I can love him. And I can pray for him. But I cannot help him. The proof: anyone with whom I'm emotionally involved and whom I'm trying to help is probably worse off today than the day I first started trying to help him.

That was one of the points I shared with the gentleman who called. Now I get to put it in this book.

To repeat: once you're sober, ain't life grand? ■

Q. What Is Cross Talk and Why Can't I Do It?

A. One of the nicest things about Twelve Step meetings is, unlike everywhere else on the planet, people don't interrupt each other. Not only that, you could put your hand up and speak for two or three minutes, and no matter how dumb, trivial, or useless your share might be, everyone will either thank you or give you a round of applause.

How great is that?

Seriously, it's fantastic that there is little to no cross talk in Twelve Step meetings. *Cross talk* means giving advice to another person, or commenting directly on a prior share in the meeting. Humility dictates that we don't cross talk. After all, if we were so smart, we would never have become alcoholics and addicts in the first place. We don't have all the answers for ourselves, so why do we suddenly think we have all the answers for other people?

On top of that, there's a chilling effect if it's clear that people are going to comment on what members have to say. It feels safe when they know that their message will neither be interrupted nor criticized. In some meetings in New York City, the leader comments on whatever each member just shared, often in an impenetrable if charmingly streetwise outer-borough accent. In those meetings, I sometimes ask the leader not to comment on what I have to say.

The main thing is that we alcoholics and addicts are people who don't feel safe anywhere when we first get sober—with the exception of meetings. So it's up to us to create and maintain an environment for newcomers so that they feel comfortable enough to speak without worrying.

No cross talk is pretty cool. ▪

Q. What Should I Share in a Twelve Step Meeting?

A. If you're new, you don't have to share. The Twelve Step meetings were meant to be like the classroom, where the people with time share their experience, strength, and hope about recovery. You are under no obligation to speak.

In some old-school AA meetings, there's a very strong bias against newcomers speaking. In one of my favorite meetings, the Sunday morning men's group in Lynn, Massachusetts, when newcomers start professing about recovery, when clearly they don't know much, the other members start dropping quarters on their metal folding chairs as a sign of protest. It gets worse. The next person to speak will raise his hand and ask a rhetorical question: "What should a newcomer do in a meeting of Alcoholics Anonymous?"

(If you really want to have fun, read the following responses out loud with a strong north-of-Boston accent.)

Another person will raise his hand and say, "He should keep his mouth shut and his ears open and try to learn something."

The next person will say, "He shouldn't say anything. If we need to know about alcoholism, we'll call on him. Otherwise, he should just try to fill a seat."

And the next person, and the next person, and the next person, will voice grave displeasure at the idea of a newcomer going on too long.

It's funny, but it can be a little unnerving, so don't put your hand up in the Lynn Men's Meeting until you've been around a while. Sometimes the newcomer is so insulted that he doesn't come back, which is never the intention. The serious point is that you are not obligated to speak. Discussion meetings in most Twelve Step groups can turn into what my friend and AA archivist Wally P. calls "group therapy sessions without a therapist." Such discussions help no one and can actually be dangerous. If you are talking about your feelings and no one says anything, because of the rule against cross talk, you can end up feeling worse than if you had never said anything at all.

The best thing to talk about in a Twelve Step program is something that will give hope and sustenance to the newcomer. You might say, "But I *am* the newcomer!" The reality is that other newcomers will listen to you far more carefully than they will to the old-timers. First, they don't relate to the old-timers as much as they relate to a fellow newcomer. They may think the old-timers are lying about how much time they really have. The story goes that the newcomer turned to the person on his left and said, "How much time do you have?"

"Ten years."

Whereupon the newcomer turned to the person on his right and asked, "How much time do *you* have?"

"Ten days."

"How did you do it?" the newcomer asks the guy with ten days.

You get the point—if you have been sober for only a short amount of time, your experience of staying sober is going to be more powerful than the experience of the person with a lot of time. It may sound perverse, but it's true. So keep in mind that if you share about your problems, you will help no one, probably not even yourself. But if you share a solution on any level—any sort of hope that things are going to get better for you because you are working this Twelve Step program—you will give hope to the next person. You will help save that person's life. And isn't that why we're in the meeting in the first place? ■

Q. I'm *Really* Not Supposed to Date for a Whole Year? You *Kidding* Me?

A. That's what they say.

We're not trying to cut into your enjoyment of life. We are saying that the emotions present in a new relationship, high and low, all too often trigger the impulse to drink and use.

An extremely famous movie star, whose name I cannot reveal due to anonymity considerations, once told me his favorite Twelve Step acronym. It is RELATIONSHIP, and it stands for Really Exciting Love Affair Turns Into Outrageous Nightmare; Sobriety Hangs In Peril.

You gotta love it. That really sums it up. A new love relationship, or a new sexual relationship, or, since we're talking about addicts and alcoholics, a new hostage-taking relationship, is just too thrilling. There's such excitement around the idea of potentially having found *The One*.

We've seen over and over again that a new relationship jeopardizes one's commitment to sobriety. Aside from the emotional roller coaster, there's also the time element. Newcomers need to go to a lot of meetings. The hostage, er, new flame isn't always that interested in meetings. Or doesn't like meetings. Or, worse still for your sobriety, doesn't see why *you* need to go to meetings.

Really exciting love affair turns into outrageous nightmare. Before long, sobriety really does hang in peril.

The old-timers used to say, "Behind every skirt is a slip."

Maybe today we would amend that to say that behind every pair of boxers is a blow to your sobriety.*

Another consideration is that alcoholics and addicts tend to get into relationships so that they don't have to have a relationship with themselves. It sounds like a cliché, but it's true. You've got to take care of you. You've got to get to know yourself. You've got to figure out who you are, now that the disease is no longer driving the bus. It's hard to do that when a new relationship is a distraction and a time sump.

Of course, this may well be the single most ignored piece of guidance offered in Twelve Step meetings. It's one thing to be told that you can't drink, inject, swallow, or snort. It's another thing altogether to be told that you ought to get out of the sex business.

Consider, however, that just as water finds its own level, so do people in relationships. You will neither be attracted to nor attractive to anyone at a higher spiritual level than where you are right now. And if you are new, your spirit is jacked. Getting into a relationship in early recovery is almost begging for addiction to kick in again. I'm a big fan of Terry Gorski. His books and audio have been really enlightening for me. Gorski has often covered the idea that it's really tough on people to bounce from one pain-filled relationship to the next, or to oscillate between a painful relationship and painful loneliness. Without getting off that ride, we're only setting ourselves up for painful togetherness followed by painful separation. This is certainly advice I ignored in my first year. I guess I'm just passing it along as a public service. Since you know better, I have no doubt that you'll ignore it, too. ■

---

*What's that sound? Why, it's my editor cringing, 1,500 miles from here.

A. Probably.

Most people are resilient and want to put the past behind them. Whatever damage we did was done; we cannot un-ring the bell. But one of the biggest gifts our sobriety provides is that we do not continue to hurt people the way we have hurt them in the past. This is for two reasons: First, when we are active in the program, we reduce the level of pain we have inside us, pain we dish out on other people. Second, the awareness that our sobriety hinges on making amends for when we harm people acts as a governor on our behavior. At some point, the realization kicks in that if I say or do something harmful, I will have to apologize for it. Rather than have to apologize, I simply don't do the harmful thing in the first place.

This is called maturity.

Sometimes addicts and alcoholics say to themselves, "What's the point? They'll never forgive me."

Warning: This is your disease speaking to you. It's telling you that things never change for the better, so why not drink or use?

Don't listen to that siren song. It's a dirty lie. I have seen so many marriages, family relationships, and love relationships of all kinds restored through active application of the Twelve Steps. Stick around and the same thing will most likely happen to you.

It's not a guarantee—we cannot control what other people say or do. I don't think everyone I hurt forgave me, even when I made my amends. For the most part, though, people really do want to prove William Faulkner wrong when he said, "The past is never dead. It's not even past."

It's a defeatist attitude to believe that relationships cannot improve. You may not get a particular relationship back, whether it's a marriage or anything else, but you just might. And if anything, while you may not always be able to make things better, you certainly will not be making anything worse. ▨

Q. Is It Okay to Talk about Drugs in an AA Meeting?

A. Strictly speaking, we are supposed to refer only to alcohol in meetings of Alcoholics Anonymous and whatever narcotics we were involved with in Narcotics Anonymous meetings and so on.

Not too many people feel this way anymore, but since you've asked, that's the reality.

Every meeting's culture is different. Some, dominated by the crusty old-timers I've mentioned throughout this book, will caution or even silence a member who speaks about drugs.

In others, as long as you preface your remarks with "I know this is AA, but . . ." no one seems to mind. And in still more meetings, nobody cares, period.

For me, the issue comes down to diluting the program. The Traditions tell us that "Alcoholics Anonymous has no opinion on outside issues," and since alcohol is the focus of AA, drugs are an outside issue. It's hard for some newcomers, whose alcoholism is so deeply entwined with drug abuse, to separate the two and only speak about alcoholism in AA. The concern is that since AA is only about alcoholism, talking about drugs will water the program down.

Chances are, unless you yourself are a crusty old-timer, you really couldn't care less whether people speak about drugs in the meeting. And if you are a crusty old-timer, it's really neat that you've read this far into a book about the first three Steps! So there may be hope for you yet. ■

Do I Have to Tell People I'm Working a Program?

A. It's said that an extrovert is someone to whom nothing really happens until he tells about it. Or maybe we just live in a world of Oprah-like compulsive over-sharing.

Either way, you don't have to tell anybody that you're in a Twelve Step program. Remember that the last name of almost every Twelve Step fellowship, with the exception of Al-Anon, is Anonymous. In AA and other Twelve Step programs, we think highly of alcoholics and addicts, because that's what we are, too. We recognize our common struggle, our common humanity, and our common solution.

Out there, people don't like us. Addicts and alcoholics are considered undependable, unreliable, dishonest, two-timing, selfish, and thoughtless. In the meetings, we laugh at the scrapes we get ourselves and other people into. Out there, nobody's laughing.

So you don't have to tell anyone that you've entered a Twelve Step program. It's really not their business. What matters, going forward, is how you behave, how you treat people if they do know that you are in a recovery fellowship. As the expression goes, you may be the only copy of the Big Book they see that day. So they may well be judging the sincerity and effectiveness of the program by how you act.

This doesn't mean that you have to suddenly sprout a halo and wings and always do things perfectly. It does mean that if you're going to tell people that you're clean and sober, that you've turned a new leaf, and that you've found a new spiritual path, you'd better act like a decent person. If you're going to be the Messiah, don't make a mess.

Pretty much everyone in my world knows that I'm sober in AA—everyone in my extended family, all of my friends, and even most of my coworkers. I'm open about my anonymity for two reasons: First, when I was new, I started telling people because it meant that they would be less likely to offer me a drink. And second, they can use me as a resource—if they or anyone they know needs Twelve Step recovery, they know they can call me and ask me about it.

That's different from breaking my anonymity at the level of "press, radio, and film," as the Traditions remind us. You won't see my real last name, or my photo, on this book or in any marketing related to this book. For all you know, I'm the guy who sits next to you at your Tuesday night AA meeting. Not that guy, the one on the other side. The good-looking one.

As for breaking other people's anonymity, I just don't do it. The damage that can be caused by gossiping about fellow members is endless and sometimes irretrievable. If running my mouth means that I could harm somebody else's relationship, reputation, or career, why would I do it?

The only area where I've really faltered in this regard has to do with TV and movie stars I see in meetings. Yes, I have gossiped about them to other people in AA. We are not saints. So if you are a TV star or movie star and I gossiped about you, I apologize. You can find your name in the appendix of this book. ▨

Q. What's All This Talk about Humility, Anyway?

A. We find a reference to humility in the Seventh Step, when we "humbly asked Him to remove our shortcomings."

It's a key word in Twelve Step land, and it also bothers people. What does *humility* mean, they wonder? Does it mean groveling and telling everyone how bad you were?

No. Not in the least. The Big Book even tells us that we grovel before no one. Now that we're clean, we can hold our heads high. So what exactly is humility, and why is it such an important concept in the program?

Let's go back 2,000 years to ancient Rome. The word for ground is *humus*. The words *humility* and *humiliation* both derive from that Latin word *humus*. *Humility* means to be grounded—to know who you are and what you are. Lois Wilson, Bill's wife and a cofounder of Al-Anon, wrote in an Al-Anon pamphlet that humility simply means knowing who you are.

This is hard for alcoholics and addicts (and those who love them). We can be grandiose and self-hating at the same time, as exemplified in the indecorous phrase, "The piece of s&%* the world revolves around." The solution is to become right-sized—to see ourselves for what we truly are. Beautiful children of God, and at the same time people who are trying hard to find a new way to live.

So that's humility—just seeing yourself for who you really are.

So while humility means being grounded, *humiliation* means being driven into the ground. The consequences we bring upon ourselves when drinking or using are often humiliating—rejection, getting fired, the disappointment in the eyes of our loved ones, going to jail.

We say that addiction is humiliating while sobriety brings humility.

So there's nothing really wrong with the concept of humility, once you're clear on the distinction between humility and humiliation.

There's a story that an AA group gave one of its members an award for humility. When he accepted the award, they took it back. ■

Q. What's the Deal with "Chiming In"?

A. Newcomers, and some old-timers as well, find it strange that people in meetings will chant in unison the last few words of some of the readings.

For example, at the end of the reading of "How It Works," including the Twelve Steps, from chapter 5 of the Big Book, the meeting will recite in unison, "Could and would if He were sought."

I don't know if they pronounce the capital letter, but you get the point.

Similarly, when reading the list of things alcoholics do to change up their drinking and make it somehow successful, the members will chant "ad infinitum" at the end of that reading.

Or even more strangely, after the announcement that "who you see here, when you leave here, let it stay here," the whole meeting will erupt with, "Hear, hear," as if they had been suddenly transported to a Quaker meeting house in the eighteenth century.

So what's the deal with all that? Why do people do it?

Clancy I., whom I've mentioned is one of the most influential old-timers in Southern California, offers the only sensible explanation I've ever heard. According to Clancy, many years ago, there was a drinking alcoholic, as opposed to a sober one, who attended meetings in the San Fernando Valley area just north of Los Angeles. He would chime in, all by himself, at the end of the readings, for reasons he never shared with anyone (possibly because he was drunk). So others in the group started to do it, to make fun of him.

Somehow, the concept spread, and now alcoholics across the fruited plain will chime in on the last few words of various readings, without ever even wondering why they do it.

And they certainly have no idea that they are emulating people who were making fun of a drunk in an AA meeting north of Los Angeles many decades earlier.

I bring this up for a reason. To my mind, anything that turns a Twelve Step meeting into a ceremony with wacky rituals is a bad idea. It's hard enough for the newcomer to sit through a meeting without jumping out of his skin. Now on top of sitting there, we're asking him to sit through weird rites that make the whole room sound like a bunch of automatons?

Isn't that what he's afraid of in the first place?

If I could change one thing in Twelve Step recovery,* well, it probably wouldn't be this. But if I could change two or three, I would get rid of the chanting and the chiming in. It makes no sense.

Hear, hear!

---

*This is the last time I'll mention the "one thing" I'd change in Twelve Step recovery. I promise.

Q. What Is Thirteenth Stepping, and Why Should I Be Concerned about It?

A. One of the troubling things about Twelve Step meetings is that they are often happy hunting grounds for lonely hearts who all too often prey on newcomers, mostly female, but occasionally male as well.

Hitting on a person with less than a year of sobriety is considered bad form.

Individuals in their first year—maybe you are one of them—are often vulnerable and lonely. Tell me, while you have been trying to figure out this recovery thing, have you been feeling pretty raw and on your own? Chances are the answer is yes. There might be others in your meeting, some of whom have considerable time and even acclaim within the fellowship, who might consider people like you "fair game."

Humping and dumping a newcomer is ugly behavior.

Twelve Step meetings must be safe places for people who find life unsafe. If we cannot provide our new members with the security of knowing that long-timers (and by that I mostly mean creepy older guys) aren't going to try to talk them into having sex, we're doing something wrong.

So if someone tries to thirteenth Step you, name his game. You can ask, "Isn't it a tradition that you're not supposed to ask out someone in her first year? Doesn't that make you into a creepy, perverted guy?"

Watch the old-timer duck away in shame. It's just not cool. ▪

Q. Will You Tell Me the Story about You and the Sex Addict?

A. I was afraid you'd ask me that.

When I was about four years sober, I asked out a girl in AA. It's the one and only time I ever asked out a girl in AA, and it took me almost twenty years to be able to tell this story.

She was really cute, and we went out to dinner or a movie or somewhere. I was driving her back to her house, and suddenly she said the six words no man wants to hear: "I've got something to tell you."

It's never anything good.

Usually it means that she's suddenly remembered that she has a boyfriend, and your audition to replace that boyfriend failed.

In this case, she told me something entirely different. "I'm a sex addict," she said.

Just another reward of the program, I thought, offering a silent prayer of thanks to my wonderfully thoughtful Higher Power.

"No problem," I said, and I was just happy to get the words out without my voice cracking like a teenager going through puberty.

"But there's something else I have to tell you," she said, and I wondered, how much better can this get?

A beautiful girl who has to have tons of sex. How great is life? What's next, threesomes? Furry animals? Talk about getting lucky!

"I'm just not that into you," she said.

Sigh.

True story. ■

Q. What if I *Still* Don't Like Meetings?

A. The relevant cliché: you only have to go to meetings until you want to go to meetings.

Then you don't have to go anymore.

Seriously, there's a lot not to like. The occasional power-driving old-timer. Boring shares. Lousy coffee.

At the same time, where else are you going to find the potential for freedom from alcohol and substances, friendship, maybe even (after your first year) romance and a new job?

It's the best deal in town for a buck, and you don't even have to put anything into the collection basket if you don't have it or you don't feel like it.

You may not like Twelve Step meetings, but realistically, what's the alternative? Drinking and using in moderation? Getting fired from another job? Getting dumped in another relationship?

And we both know it only gets worse from there.

There's no law that says you have to like it, but there's a very strong chance that if you stick around, you'll come to appreciate it.

There are so many alcoholic or addicted ways to die. You can choke on your own vomit. You can shoot yourself, intentionally or unintentionally. You can drive your car the wrong way on the highway.

As we've said,* you cannot scare an alcoholic or an addict, but if you're planning to stick around for a while at Twelve Step

---

*The royal we, of course.

recovery, buy a black suit. That's because there'll be plenty of other people out there doing research and development for you, with predictably disastrous results.

We've also said that people who don't go to meetings don't find out what happens to people who don't go to meetings. So you might as well stick around, because you don't have to run scared to get clean and sober, but a little healthy fear couldn't hurt. ■

Q. What if I *Still* Don't Like God?

A. I had a friend who went to meetings every day for two years and said the same thing every day for two years: "I don't like God."

Then one day he "got the God thing."

Thereafter, he would say every time he shared, "If you have trouble with the God thing, get over it."

All I can suggest is you keep an open mind. One of the concepts in chapter 4 of the Big Book, "We Agnostics," is that eras in which new ideas are accepted witness fantastic change and growth.

Ask any longshoreman, Bill wrote, about whether a trip to the moon could take place one day, and the answer will be in the affirmative.

Of course, this was written thirty years before men went to the moon.

Success, in short, comes from a willingness to exchange old ideas for new ones. The Steps stress coming to terms with a Higher Power. But there's no rush. You've got the rest of your life to figure out the whole God thing and decide whether you want to substitute your old ideas about a Higher Power for new ones. In the end, as they say, just fill a seat.

You'll get the God thing eventually. Or the God thing will get you.

A. I would invoke the tough noogie rule. It's just tough noogies on them.

Sometimes newcomers find it illogical that their loved ones would not want them to get clean and sober. But there are surprising reasons. One is control. Addicts and alcoholics are remarkably, even delightfully, easy to control. When we get sober, it can be a challenge for the partner who doesn't drink or use, because suddenly that person has to share power in the relationship as never before.

There's something consistent and predictable about the behavior patterns of a practicing addict or alcoholic. When we get clean, we confound those expectations and complicate the lives of our partners. They don't always like it.

The second issue may be that our partner or partners have struggled, often for years, to induce us to become sober. Through bribery, through pleading, through manipulation, through cunning, and through withholding of love or sex, they were determined to induce sobriety in us, without success.

And here comes a roomful of strangers, able to accomplish what they could not.

It can be frustrating for them, but my sympathy has its limits. To my mind, your sobriety and abstinence come first. If you are not going to meetings, exactly what good will you be in your relationship?

Your partner may also resent the amount of time that the program takes. You may be out evening after evening, going to coffee, spending time with your sponsor, and doing all the things that a recovering alcoholic or addict must do in order to have a shot at sobriety. This time has to come from somewhere, and often it comes from the time that you spent with your partner.

Your program must come first. If you drink or use, it is a stone-cold lock that eventually you will lose your relationship, your job, your children, your dignity, and all the other things that matter in life. If your relationship is not strong enough to withstand your sobriety, it is almost certainly not strong enough to survive your continued drinking and using.

So be sensitive to the concerns of your partner. Whether he or she misses the control over you that he or she once enjoyed, resents your fellow addicts and alcoholics who helped you get clean, or resents you for being out at all those meetings, or some combination thereof, it doesn't matter. Anything you put ahead of your program, you'll lose. So keep your program in the number one slot, and eventually everything else will sort itself out.

You could offer to attend an Al-Anon meeting with your partner. Why should we alcoholics and addicts have all the fun? ■

Q. Now Tell Me the Story about Your Sponsee Kevin, Okay?

A. Okay, here goes.

The first time Kevin asked me to sponsor him, I said no. I was physically afraid of him. He had a malevolent gleam in his eye, and I just thought, this guy's trouble.

I was about three years sober, and we ran into each other most weeks on the T, the trolley line that took us both to different meetings we attended at a particular church in Brookline, Massachusetts. This is more than twenty-two years ago.

He asked again, and since we're not supposed to say no to an AA request, I agreed. His eyes lit up.

"You sponsah the monstah!" he said, with his pronounced Boston accent.

Like I said, his name was Kevin. He'd been a high-flier on Wall Street in the eighties and then crashed and burned, a cocaine cowboy and a casualty of the high life. A veteran who, if he was to be believed, had seen plenty of combat in Vietnam in the 1970s, he had a hard time staying clean. To his credit, every time he picked up, he somehow found his way back to a meeting.

He wasn't a monster. He was smart, thoughtful, extremely well read, and curious. When I went through a breakup with a fiancée, he insisted on seeing me every day. He was worried about me.

And then one day, life became too hard for him, and he decided he would end it all.

He and another drunk shared a bottle of Listerine on a five-degree Boston winter night. Kevin wanted to kill himself, but he didn't want his daughter to think he was a suicide, so he figured that he would freeze to death and his motives would be forever obscured.

Morning came. The Boston police found the two men. The other one was dead. Kevin still had a pulse, so they took him to Boston City Hospital, where he was intubated and comatose. The law of Massachusetts is that you cannot declare a frozen person dead until you have tried to heat him up. Kevin had a core body temperature of seventy-nine degrees. His nurses told me that no one had ever survived after having been admitted to their hospital with such a low core body temperature.

Kevin remained in a coma for thirty days. When he regained consciousness, the chaplain came to visit him. "Is there a person of your faith you'd like to see?"

"I want to see my AA sponsor, Mike." He somehow managed to rattle off my phone number.

The chaplain called me and told me the story. I went to see him.

Kevin looked like someone you see in a photograph of Holocaust survivors. His robust physique was gone—he must have lost all of his muscle mass through his ordeal—and his teeth were missing. I felt as though I were talking to a ghost.

"You think I'm constitutionally incapable of getting this thing?" Kevin asked. I remember thinking that I didn't have the right answer.

"I don't think so," I said. "I think you just like to drink and use."

I can still see in my mind's eye Kevin mulling that answer over and then nodding in agreement.

He knew he wouldn't be leaving the hospital for a while, so he asked me to bring a book for him to read—Thomas Flanagan's *The Year of the French.*

It's a very fine novel. I told you Kevin was a smart guy.

Little by little, Kevin's recovery began. Since he was a veteran, he was able to receive treatment and shelter at various VA facilities in the Boston area. I didn't have a car back then, so I would take several buses to go see him at one facility and then another. He was clean and sober, going to meetings, and putting his life back together. He was regaining his physical strength—he was so excited when he could do a pull-up again.

He got a new set of teeth.

We went to get his driver's license. That was a moment of triumph for him.

Finally, he was able to get a subsidized studio apartment in Beacon Hill. I never visited him there—he was probably ashamed of how small it was—but it was home.

He even gave me the draft of the novel he wrote, about a Vietnam veteran who went to Wall Street and got into drugs.

Kevin worked the Steps and chose to do his Fifth Step with a priest. I couldn't argue with that, but I did feel miffed. I wasn't good enough? But how can you argue when a sponsee tells you he wants to do his Fifth Step with a priest?

We went to meetings all over town together, and it was fun. As I said, Kevin was smart and thoughtful. He just had a terrible disease.

Which finally took him out. In the mid- to late 1990s, I've since learned, the purity of heroin available on the streets suddenly shot upward. It was so much stronger than anything people had seen before. People were dying by the droves.

And then it was Kevin's turn. I forget now how I got the news, but somebody called me and told me that Kevin had overdosed on heroin—as if there's a good, healthy "dose" and he simply missed the mark. And that was the end of the story, or so I thought.

A few years later, I was living in Los Angeles and newly engaged (to a different woman, of course). I got a letter in the mail. This was the 1990s, before email destroyed the gentle art of letter writing.

It was a letter from Kevin's daughter, the one from whom he had wanted to hide his suicidal impulses by sharing that bottle of Listerine on that five-degree Boston night.

She wanted to know about her father, and she had some questions for me. How she found me, and how she found my California address, I have no idea.

She lived in Washington, D.C., and if I ever visited Washington, she would love to meet me and ask about her father.

I'm never in Washington, D.C. I have no business there. I have a few friends, and some family, but I never go there.

With one exception.

My fiancée and I were flying there that same weekend to attend a cousin's wedding.

I called her and we made a meeting time at Washington's Union Station. She was eighteen and as sweet as could be. Once we sat down, she got right to the point.

"You knew my father," she said. "Did he ever mention to you whether he molested me? I have no idea if it happened, and I need to know."

Astonished by the question, I found myself in the same position as I had been at Boston City Hospital, when Kevin, toothless and rail thin, asked me if he was constitutionally incapable of getting this thing.

I thought back, and I keenly regretted the fact that he had not done his Fifth Step with me, because then I could have given a definitive answer.

"He never said anything of the sort," I said. "I knew your father well. I know he did a lot of bad things, but he always spoke about how much he loved you. I can tell you with certainty that it never happened."

She looked relieved. We spoke for a few more minutes and went our separate ways. I haven't seen her since.

How could I be so sure? I couldn't. But what I told her was

true—he had never said anything about that, and we talked about everything under the sun, as open and honest as two men can be. It nagged at me—maybe that's why he needed to talk to a priest instead of me. I'll never know.

You can debate the legitimacy of my definitive answer. Reasonable minds may differ. But in reality in my heart, I didn't believe that he had done it. So why share doubts I didn't have? If you would have handled the situation differently, that's fine, but that's how I did it.

I tell you this story because every year on my anniversary, I dedicate my coin to Kevin's memory. He was a profound friend, and I treasured and still treasure our relationship. But the real reason I tell you this story is because now I have four children, including two daughters, and I never, ever, ever want any of my children to have to track down one of my AA sponsors and ask him what kind of person I was.

I once heard a girl in a meeting say, "If you drank once with me, you knew I was an alcoholic. If you drank twice with me, I knew you were, too."

If you talk with me once about sobriety, you'll see how serious I am about it. If you talk twice with me about sobriety, I'll know you're just as serious.

You must be, because you've come along on this journey with me. I hope that I've reduced some of the mystery and confusion surrounding Twelve Step recovery. I hope I've answered some of your questions and paved the way for you to find the people who can answer the rest.

I owe everything important in my life—my marriage, my four children, my sense of self-worth, my spiritual life, my health, my freedom, and my identity—to the Twelve Step programs of which I am a member. I hope that you find what I've found, and that's why I wrote this book. ■

Q. Can We Do the Poem Now?

A. Sure.

When I was in my first year, I heard a speaker named Bob L., a legend in southern California AA, speak at the Marina Center in west Los Angeles. He told an amazing story about how he loved being a police officer and then one day, in a drunken stupor, he pulled his service revolver on his wife.

That was the end of his career.

Bob L. has one of the most powerful messages I've ever heard, and you could do a lot worse than tracking him down on one of the websites that aggregate Twelve Step speaker audios. He would conclude every talk he gave with a poem, a copy of which he says he found at his first meeting.

He swears that that poem kept him sober, which is why he recites it. I'll share it with you now.

Which Place?[4]
I dreamed one night I passed away and left this world behind.
I started down that rocky trail, some of my friends to find.
I came to a signpost on that trail. Directions it did tell:
"Turn right to go to heaven. Turn left to go to hell."
I hadn't been too good on Earth, just a hopeless, boozing rake.
So I knew at the crossroads which path I'd have to take.
Started down that rocky path that leads to Satan's place
and shook within! Not knowing just what I'd have to face.

Old Satan met me at the gate. "What's your name, my friend?"
I said, "I'm just old Sober Sam, that's come to a sad end."
He checked through his files. "There's been a mistake, I fear.
You're listed as an alcoholic. We don't want you here."
I told him I was looking for some friends, and a smile crept over
     his face.
"If your friends are alcoholic, they're in the other place."
So I turned back the other way, till crossroads I did see
And then turned straight for heaven, as happy as could be.
Saint Peter smiled and said, "Come in. For you we have a berth.
You're an alcoholic. You've been through hell on earth."
I saw Old Pete and Dub, too, and a gal named Belle, and brother,
     I was tickled
Because I thought they'd gone to hell.
So brothers (and sisters) take warning. Learn something from
     this trip.
There's a place for you in heaven if you try hard not to slip.
And if someone offers you a drink when you're not feeling well,
Tell him you're going to heaven, and he can go to hell!

APPENDIX

Q.

*Michael, tell me about all the
famous movie stars you've seen in
meetings and gossiped about.*

A.

*Yeah, like I'm really going to do that
in this book. Sorry.*

Notes and Suggested Readings

1. Joe and Charlie: The Internet is full of material from Joe and Charlie. People frequently download audio and content from Twelve Step speaker sites. To learn more about Joe and Charlie, check out the following article: https://www.thefix .com/content/legend-joe-and-charlie6008?page=all.

2. Terry Gorski, audio recordings from talks, circulated in the 1990s. Terry is internationally recognized for his contributions to the recovery community. A prolific writer, trainer, and speaker, his work has meant a lot to me as a person in recovery and as an author. Check out his books and audio recordings.

3. Al-Anon Family Groups, *Alcoholism, the Family Disease* (New York: World Services).

4. The Poem: AA speaker Bob L. says he found a photocopy of "Which Place?" (often referred to as "The Poem") "in the rooms," circa 1964. There's no record of who wrote it or when, but it's still widely shared today. With gratitude and respect for the author, I share the message.

Acknowledgments

Let's start with Vanessa Torrado, my fabulous editor, who has been the dream publishing partner since our first encounter. Vanessa saw the value in my work and is responsible for the existence of this book as well as *Sober Dad* and the books to follow. Her instincts are superb, her editing is Maxwell Perkins–level, and her knowledge of the publishing industry is unmatched. She is a gift from my Higher Power.

I'd also like to acknowledge the equally fabulous Don Freeman, April Ebb, Terri Kinne, Heather Silsbee, Wendy Videen, Alison Vandenberg, Emily Reller, Susan Whitten, Jody K., and Jill Grindahl for making the book a reality and helping it get into your hands.

Amy Spahn typed the manuscript and made me look better as a writer than I really am.

My sincere thanks to Harv, Jan, and Andy A., who sponsored me in Al-Anon, and to Steve M., who sponsors me today in Overeaters Anonymous. I talk to Steve daily, and he is a huge gift in my life.

Above all, I'm grateful to Bill W. and Dr. Bob, whose ever-widening circle of peace on earth came to include my family and yours.

About the Author

"Michael Graubart" is a longtime sober member of Alcoholics Anonymous, has been a member of Al-Anon for decades, and attends Overeaters Anonymous meetings as well. As he says, "If it moves, I'm obsessed with it, and if it stands still, I'm addicted to it." A *New York Times* best-selling author, Michael is married and the father of four children. He's the author of *Sober Dad: The Manual for Perfectly Imperfect Parenting,* as well as an accomplished singer-songwriter who has recently released his first CD of songs about recovery, titled *Sober Songs, Volume I.*

Following the Traditions, he writes under a pseudonym to maintain his anonymity. For all you know, he's the good-looking guy who sits next to you at one of your meetings. Anonymity helps him speak frankly about his experiences in Twelve Step recovery.

Stay in touch with him on social media and through his site **MichaelGraubart.com.**

About Hazelden Publishing

As part of the Hazelden Betty Ford Foundation, Hazelden Publishing offers both cutting-edge educational resources and inspirational books. Our print and digital works help guide individuals in treatment and recovery, and their loved ones. Professionals who work to prevent and treat addiction also turn to Hazelden Publishing for evidence-based curricula, digital content solutions, and videos for use in schools, treatment programs, correctional programs, and electronic health records systems. We also offer training for implementation of our curricula.

Through published and digital works, Hazelden Publishing extends the reach of healing and hope to individuals, families, and communities affected by addiction and related issues.

For more information about Hazelden publications,
please call **800-328-9000**
or visit us online at **hazelden.org/bookstore.**

OTHER TITLES THAT MAY INTEREST YOU

Drop the Rock: Removing Character Defects
Second Edition

BILL P., TODD W., and SARA S.

Based on the principles behind Steps Six and Seven, *Drop the Rock* combines personal stories, practical advice, and powerful insights to help readers move forward in recovery.

Order No. 4291 (softcover); also available as an ebook.

Drop the Rock—The Ripple Effect: Using Step Ten to Work Steps Six and Seven Every Day

FRED H., foreword by WILLIAM C. MOYERS

In this follow-up to *Drop the Rock: Removing Character Defects*, Fred H. explores "the ripple effect" that can be created by using Step Ten to practice Steps Six and Seven every day.

Order No. 9743 (softcover); also available as an ebook.

Practicing the Here and Now: Being Intentional with Step 11

HERB K.

With *Practicing the Here and Now*, you'll find the guidance needed to approach prayer and meditation as practices to help you be present throughout each day, as you remain in contact with your Higher Power for ongoing inspiration and sustenance.

Order No. 8996 (softcover); also available as an ebook.

Keep It Simple: Daily Meditations for Twelve-Step Beginnings and Renewal

The meditations in this best-selling classic focus on the Twelve Steps, stressing the importance of putting into practice new beliefs, slogans, and fellowship.

Order No. 5066 (softcover); also available as an ebook.